To y
beautiful
magic,

(signature)

Just Give Me Meaningful Work

JUST GIVE ME MEANINGFUL WORK

ESCAPE YOUR EXHAUSTING JOB AND START MAKING A DIFFERENCE

JULIE P. BOYER

NEW YORK

LONDON • NASHVILLE • MELBOURNE • VANCOUVER

Just Give Me Meaningful Work

Leave Your Exhausting Job and Start Making a Difference

Published in New York, New York, by Morgan James Publishing in partnership with Difference Press. Morgan James is a trademark of Morgan James, LLC. www.MorganJamesPublishing.com

The Morgan James Speakers Group can bring authors to your live event. For more information or to book an event visit The Morgan James Speakers Group at www.TheMorganJamesSpeakersGroup.com.

ISBN 9781642790054 paperback
ISBN 9781642790061 eBook
Library of Congress Control Number: 2018935554

Cover Design by:
Paul Curtis

Interior Design by:
Christopher Kirk
www.GFSstudio.com

In an effort to support local communities, raise awareness and funds, Morgan James Publishing donates a percentage of all book sales for the life of each book to Habitat for Humanity Peninsula and Greater Williamsburg.

Get involved today! Visit
www.MorganJamesBuilds.com

To my four nieces:

May you always know your magic,
and that you change the world just by being you.

Table of Contents

Introduction:
Trapped in the Wrong Job

For the third time in the last 30 minutes, Mel reaches behind her, without lifting her head from the pillow or opening her eyes, and slaps the snooze button. Her husband drops his belt as he dresses, and it lands on the wood floor with a clap. Mel moans audibly in irritation.

"It's not like you don't have to get up...." he mutters, and leaves for the gym. Mel manages to open her eyes, and pull herself up. She sits on the edge of the bed, stretching out the kink in her neck, dreading today's meeting with her boss. She considers everything else on her plate today: the proposal she has to put together; the mounting excess of bureaucratic paperwork she's been avoiding. And she tells herself: *Just get through the day.*

There's no time for a workout, so Mel showers, dresses, and puts her makeup on. She doesn't have the motivation to put breakfast together, so she heads to her favorite café for a croissant.

"Hey Joe. Hey Angie," she says as she approaches the counter. It's the first time she smiles today, and she means it. Those two make her so happy. *Do they love their job? Is* that *why they always seem happy?* she wonders. She chats with Joe about her weekend as he makes her cappuccino. When she sits down and takes her first sip, she feels a surge of warmth run through her. As she bites into her croissant and stares out the window, she recalls that trip to France she took after college. She remembers the rush of traveling on her own, the sensory explosion that the food brought, how inspired she felt while reading in cafés, and how her mood miraculously shifted every time she entered a cathedral. How she'd love to go back instead of facing her boss today.

Instead, she pulls out her phone and checks her emails. Within seconds, her whole being changes. Her mind starts racing, and she notices that she's wasting time. She rushes to the office and starts her workday, making sure to check her calendar at least once every hour. This is to remind herself that there are only five weeks until she and her husband go to St. John – and that moment couldn't come soon enough. She feels a pang of guilt, however, knowing how cranky she's been with her husband lately. She cringes at this realization. She hasn't been herself in a long time; her unhappiness at work has taken its toll on both of them.

But what am I supposed to do? she thinks. *I'm stuck here.* On paper, her life looks great, and her income gives her more stability than most people have. But her work means little to her, and it's hard to live with that. She can't seem to shut off the nagging feeling that she's capable of something more, a job where she could actually make a difference, one that would make her feel proud at the end of the day. She's almost embarrassed to say she's a project manager, but it's not like she knows what work she should be doing. She's bored, irritated, and mad at herself for not being able to lift herself out of this rut.

By 11am, Mel is exhausted and considering a second cup of coffee. Looking at her phone, she realizes she doesn't have enough time before meeting with her boss, so she grabs a water bottle, hoping that will help. Waiting for her boss to arrive in the conference room, she finds herself fantasizing about getting laid off. She pictures herself packing her belongings into a box, giving everyone hugs, and leaving while the sun is still shining. She imagines going home to take a nap. *OMG, a nap*, she thinks.

She's too distracted by this fantasy of escape when her boss sits down and makes small talk with her, but whatever he's saying, she's pretty sure she's heard it before. Soon Mel notices her boss is smiling, and she tunes back into the conversation. Far from being laid off, he's praising her accomplishments; what he's trying to say is that she is getting promoted.

What happens next for Mel confuses her. Her skin goes numb, and a wash of fatigue – like a trillion-pound tidal wave – rushes over her. As her eyes glaze, she notices the effort it takes to keep them open. She feels a mix of horror and embarrassment as she watches herself force a smile. She hopes her emotions aren't all over her face for her boss to see.

She manages to hear all the right words come out of her mouth. "Wonderful. I'm so happy. Thank you." She feels like a total fraud, and guilty for lying. After her meeting, she grabs her coat and walks outside, so she can call her best friend, Jill. *Please pick up, please pick up*, she thinks. Luckily, Jill answers.

"Jill," she says, as she covers her face with her hand. "What is wrong with me?"

A Predicament Like Mel's

If you're like me and you identify with Mel's story, then you know how painfully difficult it can be to stay in a job that's not right for you. For everyone else, work may be stressful at times, but you feel downright *afflicted*. There is something unbearable about going to work every day, knowing you're really only a shadow of yourself there. It doesn't matter whether you have a boss who shuts down your ideas and prevents you from having any opportunities to grow, or you feel fundamentally misaligned with the values of your company, or you're so far removed from your natural talents that your self-esteem has plummeted – the impact is the same. You feel trapped, like you're not living the life you were supposed to live.

The cost of staying stuck becomes more obvious as time marches on, but the problem doesn't get any easier to solve. You start succumbing to your toxic work environment and bringing your reactivity home with you, causing too many needless fights. You find yourself avoiding life by watching more and more television, overeating when you get home, or resorting to a glass of wine to help you relax. You're resigned to it all, and your family wonders what's happened to you. Not only are you missing the deep satisfaction of knowing and using your gifts to make an impact around you, but you seem to be stuck with the opposite. You're stuck in negative pattern, a negative attitude, and it doesn't feel right. *You know* it's not right. You're disappointing yourself. As hard as you've tried, you're still in the same place, trying to find a way out.

It can be relatively easy to know when something isn't working: You start to feel trapped, and red flags like anxiety and mood swings show up everywhere. And yet, at the same time, it can be downright scary when you realize you don't know what you want to do next, and even if you do, you have no idea how to get there.

But in your frustration, anger, boredom, and impatience there is actually hope. All of these feelings are pointing you toward the choice you want to be making – a choice that's actually available to you. Your emotions aren't here to make you miserable, they're here to tell you that you're ready for change. They're here to show you what you care about, what you've had enough of, and what you want to do with your life. Just because you haven't found a way *yet* to create the changes you're looking for doesn't mean those changes are impossible. They *are* possible. What you want for yourself – a job that feels easy because you can be yourself, one that taps your most natural strengths, one that challenges you and feeds you with a deep sense of fulfillment – is within your reach. And your journey to get there is likely much easier than you think it is. You've put in enough time struggling. Now it's time for some relief, and some real change.

Where the Struggle Begins

Mel's struggle is the story of so many of us. I've lived it in my own way, as have my clients and friends. You're not the only one who's ever been in this tunnel without a light at the end, and you don't have to stay here.

I've written this book because I believe that Mel – and you – are capable of creating the sense of fulfillment and ease at work that you wish for. In fact, not only are you capable of creating the change you want, but you're being *called* to. The frustration you've been feeling isn't a sign that your only choice is to endure and make the best of your life now. It's a sign that now is the time to discover what's holding you back, uncover what you really want, and relieve yourself of this frustration so you can do the work you're really meant to do.

I, too, have known what it's like to yearn for more but also be too tied up in knots of stress and frustration to do anything about it. I've been so stuck that I didn't feel like I knew myself anymore. I've been so frustrated that I forgot all about my natural strengths, which made me feel doubtful that I had the capacity to create any change in my life. I used to look around and see everyone else having a much easier time finding and excelling at work that fulfilled them, and wonder why, for me, this was such an indecipherable riddle.

You're not doomed to stay bored, held back, or stuck forever. As you'll see in this book, the changes you long for seem, for right now, like they're much harder and more improbable to achieve than they actually are. But all that is about to change.

My Story

Everyone encounters a moment or dramatic event in their teen years that changes their understanding of themselves and the world, and this new understanding can influence the course of your future. It doesn't have to be dramatic or qualify as traumatic in the eyes of others, but nonetheless it causes a great shift in your perception of the world. It can dictate what you think is possible and what you believe your personal limitations are. It can also be positive, for it can plant a seed for what later becomes your purpose in life. As you'll see, that certainly was true for me.

What I Learned Early On

When I was thirteen, my father got promoted, and I moved from a relaxed, casual, public school experience to a high-pressure, all-girls private school and a much more formal, upper-class neighborhood. This meant I left my entire life – community, family stability, and group of friends – at a time that was socially awkward and confusing to begin with. Since I wasn't raised with the kind of intellectual preparation my new peers had, I struggled to keep up, and lived with an intense level of underlying stress.

At the beginning of my second year there, my understanding of myself and who I needed to be in the world changed, just as I was starting to feel comfortable and relaxed. It happened when I was called into the head of middle school's office for cracking jokes in class and getting a C- on a science test. Fearing authority, and feeling like I was failing at being accepted in my new life, I decided that there was no room for a sensitive, creative, idiosyncratic nature in this new life. My teenage mind made up that it was dangerous to just be myself, for it meant I could lose all sense of belonging and community. From then on, my experience of the world became organized around my new belief that, in order to belong and in order to be loved, I had to be intellectual, I had to fit in, and I had to hide my sensitivity and idiosyncrasy.

The Confusion That Followed

I share this experience with you because it formed the basis of my struggles around finding meaningful work later in life. Instead of trusting and growing to know that my innate gifts of sensitivity, creativity, and community-building made me valuable in the working world, I operated from an ongoing sense of inadequacy. It kept me in a state of doubt and confusion. I couldn't, for the life of me, figure out how I could have a job where I could be myself and also be valued, as well as get paid. To get one, I had to give up the other: I could be myself after hours, but when it came to my career, I needed to get serious, work hard, and give everything, without regard for how it was affecting me.

Over the years, I became a martyr. And I watched my health decline. With everything I did, I gave my heart and soul: trying to make the most of it and trying to be patient and wait for the moment when I would feel proud of who I was. But I never did reach a point where I felt at ease and in my element, or like I was fulfilling my real potential through my work. Because my actions and choices were based on a flawed premise – that I had to earn my value by changing or trying to please others and wasn't of value as I was – those actions and choices led me in circles. I stayed stuck. I felt trapped, confused, and angry. *I'm more than this* I would think.

I knew viscerally that I wasn't living at my potential – work only skimmed the surface of what I knew I was capable of – and that didn't feel right to me. I couldn't say what it was, but for some reason, something always felt off. No matter what good work I was doing in the various jobs that I had – even when I had my own business – it wasn't enough. And at the same time, I'd look at my life on paper and think *I should be happy with this. Am I selfish for wanting more? Am I just self-absorbed?*

As I got older, this didn't change, and I couldn't deny that I was unhappy on the inside. The further I went down this road, the more disappointed I felt. I knew on a deep level that I wanted to make an impact on the world around me, and I wanted to experience joy and fulfillment through my work. I also wanted to feel peaceful and settled as a result. I wanted to feel good about myself. I wanted to feel like *I was* myself. I was tired of hustling and working myself to the bone, and tired of all the internal tension I felt from struggling to figure out where I belonged. The fact that I hadn't figured out where I belonged by my mid-thirties felt embarrassing.

A Pivotal Moment

Later, as a result of a culminating life crisis (which I'll describe in Chapter 10), I found my way into the coaching field. There, I miraculously found a community where I made total sense. I breathed relief, quickly and instinctively knowing I was on the right track. I didn't know exactly where coaching would lead me, or what it meant that I felt so comfortable there, but this was the right direction. I signed up for a year-long leadership intensive, which I hoped would help me break through the intimidating stack of insecurities I'd accumulated over the years that had stopped me from doing things I'd wanted to try – like leading workshops, for example.

About three-quarters of my way through the program, something happened that disrupted my understanding of myself again, and opened up the world of possibility and fulfillment I'd wanted for so long. It turned out that I wasn't crazy, selfish, or self-absorbed for wanting more. I really did have a way of making an impact in the world, and there really was a way for me to live with a deep sense of purpose and fulfillment.

The pivotal moment happened after my leadership cohort did an exercise. We were a group of about 20, and had gotten to know one another intimately. One night, without facilitation from our leaders, we were to share honest feedback about our leadership barriers and potential as individuals.

When we finished that night, there was a steady hum of tribe mates expressing how bolstered they felt, and it continued the next morning. Each person felt the tribe had seen more leadership qualities in them than they had seen in themselves, and it was empowering. There was a palpable change in the atmosphere, and it had to do with the deepened trust between everyone. Well, everyone except me.

While everyone else was on a high, I was scratching my head and drawing back emotionally in disappointment. I'd been the quiet one in the group, and it had taken a lot for me to show any vulnerability I had up until that point. I thought I'd shown myself enough for people to know me. But I hadn't felt bolstered or challenged or championed, like everyone else did as a result of that exercise. I didn't hear anything new at all, in fact. I could barely believe it, but this group didn't see me.

It was supposed to be the other way around (or so I thought): a case where others see your capacity and cause you to wake you up to it. I loved these people, which made it so disappointing to discover that they didn't see my capacity, my real gifts.

The next day, I brought it up with the group in our facilitated discussion. What came out of me then was a truth-telling about what it is like to be a highly sensitive person, why I am quiet most of the time, what I am feeling most of the time that's not evident to anyone else, and what that means to me. I talked about how I carry ginger with me for nausea, because I feel so much – and often so much of other people's feelings – that it's frequently overwhelming. I told them that I feel emotions deeply, but that doesn't at all mean that I am frail or fragile. In fact, it makes me tough. I don't shy away from experiences I want to have; I battle through them as best I can. And when I feel the feelings that are in the room, that's *data* that I'm getting. It's information. And it's important information. Being sensitive is a form of heightened perception. It isn't equal to being weak. My capacity to experience vulnerability makes me strong and scrappy, if not fearless at times. Tears flowed as I talked, and people handed me tissues. Our facilitator asked me to look around the room and see my impact. What I saw was a room full of loving eyes. I felt silence that had a yummy warmth to it. These people saw me, because I let myself be seen, and they loved me. I hadn't meant to create that impact, but by trusting them enough to reveal how I really felt, I did create one.

What followed blew my mind. At least three tribe mates approached me in the next two days to thank me. They each said, in their own way, but each with a tone of revelation, that I was speaking for them. They, too, had that level of sensitivity and had always fought it, tried to disown it, or at least ignore it. At some point they got the idea that to reveal themselves wasn't a good idea, or that they wouldn't belong if they did. I couldn't believe it. I had thought I was completely alone in this. I was so grateful for them coming forward that it still makes me cry to tell the story. I can't tell you how much I love them.

After that, I had a new understanding of myself. I could no longer hold as true that my sensitivity was a liability, and that it meant that I couldn't speak in groups or crowds, or I that I had to hide my vulnerability. I also realized that I had assumed that leaders are not vulnerable by nature. I now saw that this was wholly untrue. Vulnerability powers leadership. Vulnerability powers change. Vulnerability also powers love and connection.

As I let go of my misunderstandings about myself and my value, so much of my internal resources – ones I'd had all my life – came flooding back in. I felt as though my creativity was unleashed in a whole new way – I no longer had barriers holding me back, making everything such hard work. I remembered who I was: A core part of me that had always been there was now speaking up, and so many natural strengths and gifts resurfaced. I had a visceral knowing of what my future would be: that I would be a leader in my life, that I would create what I wanted, and that I would help others like me break out of their own limiting status quo and into their real potential.

Change Is Possible

Even though I never would have guessed how it would happen, what I wanted did happen. I got the change I was looking for, and was finally able to create work I truly loved and that made me feel great about myself. This is to say that, while you may not have any idea how you'll create the changes you want or how you'll find peace and joy in your work if that's what you're after, what you want is possible. You may, like I did, have emotional skills and instincts that you're unaware of. Your own sensitivity to emotion, heightened perception, or high standard for honesty and authenticity may be your greatest strengths. You may try to hide entire parts of yourself, thinking that they don't belong, when actually, embracing them is key to feeling at ease in your own skin.

The school I learned to fit into is in some ways a mirror of the status quo in our culture. You too may have experienced your own turning point where you decided that your emotions, your empathy toward others, or your intuition weren't as valuable as your intellect. You may now be experiencing the same frustration in your job that I experienced, and you may feel as though you could be doing more than what you are right now. You may find it impossible to let go of this nagging need for something more satisfying, work that brings you a sense of purpose and fulfillment. You may long for real connection, or to be seen, or to be comfortable in your skin, or to have a real impact on the people around you. You may, like I did, harbor secret dreams that feel so far-fetched you haven't shared them, yet at the same time you know they are real.

Why I Created This System

It's so hard to see what's stopping you when you're in this place. It feels like the world is unfairly confusing, or that it's conspiring to keep you miserable. How on earth can you imagine change from here?

You don't have to be able to imagine how you'll find the work you're meant to do, or how you'll summon the courage to try. You don't have to currently know that it's possible. I didn't, and yet I got exactly what I longed for.

In this book, I'm going to share with you the tools I've collected that will help you create the changes and experiences you long for. This group of tools is informed by my coach training at Coaches Training Institute, my experience coaching women just like you, and my own personal experiences of transformation, creativity, and change-making. Once you learn how change really works, and gain the necessary skill set, your perspective on change and how hard it is will shift. Change, as you're experiencing it now, is like trying to make potato salad with a set of woodshop tools. It just seems confusing and impossible, and you're getting hurt in the process. But once you have the right tools and put them to use, every step becomes doable. Soon you've made the potato salad, and not only do you see that it's possible for you to make potato salad, but you instantly see how you can make any salad, or soup, or casserole for that matter.

Three Essential Steps of Creating Change

If you're like I was about eight years ago, you think your situation is more complicated than most, maybe even too complicated for anyone to help you, and that finding work that's right for you may just be impossible. You know what I love about this thought? It makes what you're about to learn extra exciting!

I completely understand how hard it is to feel held back from something you want, when you're a highly intelligent person who should be able to create any change you want, let alone find a job you love. Dealing with these pesky internal barriers like fear, confusion, doubt, resistance, emotional overwhelm, and frustration – overcoming those barriers is my specialty. I understand how change works, and I've created enough miracles for myself (even healing my persistent migraines!) that I'm confident I can help you get what you want.

I've created a program to walk you through how to clear your head, firm up your intention, and feel the conviction to break out of your work and experience work you love. I've broken the process into three steps:

1. Believe that what you want is possible
2. Believe that you are capable of achieving it
3. Choose to act on your beliefs

You don't have to currently believe that getting what you want is possible. You don't have to believe you're capable of making it happen. This book will offer you all the skills you need to get there.

This isn't about willing yourself forward, or pushing or berating yourself any more than you already have. I'm not going to make you toughen up, or suck it up, or tell you to lower your standards. And, you may be surprised to know that nothing's wrong with you. You're not broken or messed up. But you are in pain, which means you're probably ready for change.

In this book, you'll learn how to overcome your fears, and you'll learn how to make life feel light and fun again, as opposed to heavy and burdensome. You'll discover easy ways to envision your future, and you'll learn to leverage feelings of joy and expectation into action. You'll connect with a place deep inside you that knows why you're here and what work you're meant to do. You'll use that clarity to – not only feel grounded and confident in your current job – but also to power your search for meaningful work. You'll tap into parts of you that you've always had but haven't fully acknowledged, and that offer you ways to make a positive impact on those around you. You'll learn how all the feelings you're feeling now are normal, and how to leverage emotional experiences for your growth. You'll learn how to look at experiences that trip you up in a way that helps you learn, heal, and move forward, so you can keep becoming the person that you know, in your heart, you can be.

If you're unhappy at work, the skills in this book will help you manage your stress and maintain your connection to what brings you joy. If you're completely stuck and desperate to leave your job, these skills will help you regain hope and envision a new future for yourself. You'll learn how to take action in ways that keep you moving forward, and keep you building positive momentum. If you're ready for any kind of change that requires growth, this book will give you the skills that make such changes possible.

Having a job that matches who you are and what you're good at, and that allows you to make a difference using these strengths, is deeply fulfilling. You will finally be seen for who you are and what you're really capable of. You'll feel great about yourself, because you'll be making a positive impact around you, just by being you. Getting to that place is a process of unveiling who you are, stripping away the barriers that hold you back, giving yourself full permission to pursue what you care about, and embracing your innate wisdom and ability to expand to meet life's challenges. With this book, I hope to ignite your passion, help you find your calling, and empower you as the person who successfully creates change in her life.

You'll find six chapters covering six different skills in depth, with exercises at the end of each for you to deepen your understanding. Read it through in order, or pick one step at a time to work with. Enjoy!

Step One in Creating Change: Believe That What You Want Is Possible

I know what it's like to want something viscerally – like a dream that follows you around and won't let you go – yet be immersed in an all-consuming struggle around that desire. It's draining to your body, spirit, and mind. If you carry this dream around with you long enough, you can become angry with yourself and quick to get angry with others. You can even start to dislike yourself. And slowly, but surely, you can even forget what is wonderful about you.

That's when you've hit bottom. When you're there, it can feel like a hole you need to dig out of. It seems like every sign and signal you get from the outside world is: *Impossible. Don't bother. You're dreaming.* Whether you're at the bottom of a hole right now, or just starting to fall in, we're going to get you out.

The first thing we're going to do to lift you out is address the most powerful – yet hidden – force that's keeping you here, which is the underlying belief that what you want isn't possible. There are probably ten or more forces creating this belief. For example, your boss may not see your potential, and may offer you little to no opportunities at work. Changing this seems completely out of your control. Your spouse, who doesn't understand why you're so unhappy, depends on you to contribute to your family income and this makes any change too risky. Your schedule is killing you, and so there's no time to even reflect on how a positive future might be possible for you. Your family's voices are in your ear, judging you for being stuck, and by now you think they may be right. And then there's your bank account. Every cent of your combined household income is accounted for, and you're afraid of what you might have to give up if you consider a career change…. Sound familiar?

These reasons for staying in a holding pattern are solid and convincing. It'd be easy to give in to them, especially when you have no real strategy to overcome them. But you don't have to.

The next three chapters will give you tools to dismantle your current belief in impossibility, lift the burden you're feeling now, and illuminate the truer perspective that what you want *is indeed possible*. You'll shake off the crusty layers of stress and exhaustion that have weighed you down and begin to source the energy, hope, and conviction that will carry you forward.

By practicing these tools, you'll master step number one in the process of change: *Believe That What You Want Is Possible*. It sounds too simple to be powerful, doesn't it? *How does that create change?* you wonder. By practicing the tools, you will soon find out.

Make Way for Possibility by Watching Your Self- Talk

*When I woke in the morning I feared what the day
would bring, so I stayed in bed
When I put my foot on the first rung of the ladder I got
scared, so I stayed on the ground
When I opened my mouth to speak, I felt the clench in
my stomach, so I remained silent
When I thought about leaving my marriage I froze, so
I stayed in helplessness
When I got out of bed I felt the sun on my face
When I climbed the ladder I saw the spectacular view
When I spoke my words I made a difference
When I left my marriage I found myself*

– Michael Wallace

If the idea that believing your dream is possible sounds like a naive and simplistic way of approaching a complicated problem like creating work that fulfills and completes you, I get it.

I've been where you are. I've experienced the impatience and frustration that comes with overcoming obstacles that seem purposely (and perfectly) designed to keep me from creating something I want. I'm not trying to sell you on magical thinking. Just the opposite. I'm going to give you tools to know how to steer clear of unconsciously and needlessly talking yourself out of your dreams before you even act on them. This chapter is all about awakening to the simple and destructive tendency we all have, to listen to the wrong voices in our heads. Then you can free yourself to make new choices.

Your thinking – the self-talk that runs inside your head, often hardly noticed – is likely making more of an impact on your life than you're aware of. Your self-talk appears to be benign enough, but that self-talk is powerful because it informs how you interpret your reality. These unconscious thoughts that you take for granted weave themselves seamlessly into your decision making. And just like that, your life is formed around them.

Not all self-talk is created equal. Some of your self-talk comes from a grounded, resilient place in you, and this voice is your friend and ally. The other kind of voice is the one that misinterprets, sounds smart and like it really knows what it's talking about, but is pure nonsense. It's like having a translator in your head who you've given explicit trust and authority, but who is essentially feeding you lies. Most of us can't tell the difference between these two different types of inner guidance unless we're taught how. You can be an extremely intelligent, self-aware person and still innocently choose to follow self-talk that leads you astray. It causes a lot of confusion! This isn't a disease. It's human nature, and a function of our survival mechanisms. But more on that later.

Seeing Through Your Self-Talk Will Empower You

When you're able to tell the difference – between self-talk that leads to expansion, confidence, and fulfillment and self-talk that leads to contraction, doubt, and frustration – you'll be empowered to make changes in your life. This simple tool, when you understand it well and use it every day, will help you see that your dream is more possible than you thought. You'll see how you've been holding yourself back without realizing it, and you'll know what to do to move forward.

When you look at how you assess whether something is worth your time or a waste of it, a good idea or a bad idea, likely or unlikely, smart or naive, safe or dangerous… all these decisions are informed by your interpretation of reality. Your self-talk is like a radio station you tune into all day, telling you how things are. It's what you look to for that interpretation.

It's a biased talk show, though. Only some of these voices on your talk-radio actually want what you want and will see opportunities. The others only look for what they fear, and have an entirely different agenda for you. They'll steer you away from opportunity. The job of these voices is to hedge all of your bets, to keep you from doing anything that will take you into new territory, or expand you, or help you grow. If what you want will change you in any way, your negative self-talk will convince you of all the reasons why you shouldn't go for it. When you hear them weighing in, it might seem like they're being selective, and that they represent logical, grounded, expert authority. They may even give you a feeling of relief sometimes. *Oh, thank goodness I'm back in control,* you'll think. That's what makes them so seductive.

In the coach training at the Coaches Training Institute, we call these negative voices *saboteurs.* Some people call them "gremlins," or "inner critics," or "your false self." No matter their name, learning who they are, where they came from, and what their purpose is will untangle the knots inside you and allow you to see clearly. Unintentionally trusting saboteur voices is the first thing I correct when working with clients, and this is why. Once my clients see through them, understand why they aren't trustworthy, and can identify them when they show up, the clients start saving themselves the trouble of getting mired in heavy feelings of doubt and helplessness. There's usually an "ah-ha" moment when things become clear. We need to teach you how to move these voices out of the way first, because no matter what other changes we get you making, if you can't spot your saboteurs and choose to ignore them, you'll find yourself going in circles.

Self-Sabotage: Where It All Begins

Saboteurs are voices that show up and say things like: *Who do you think you are?* when you're about to interview for your dream job, or *You'll never make it,* when you're pushing to make an important deadline, or *Oh why bother?* when you consider having that difficult conversation that could bring you closer to your spouse. They'll say, *You're being naïve,* when you have an idea that fills you with glee, or *You can get to it later,* when you've got a challenging task before you, or *You're living in a dream world*, when you feel like calling for a change in your office culture. They'll assure you: *You'll get eaten alive*, as you prepare a presentation for the board, or *You'll end up in the poor house,* as you consider taking a creative career path, or *You're not smart enough to handle this,* just after you get promoted. Saboteurs really sound like they know what they're talking about, because they validate our fears. Even though what they say can be overtly negative, they have a true ring of authority. They snap you out of your reverie, and into "the real world."

Saboteurs often show up when we feel out of control. Moments of vulnerability, situations that catch us off-guard, or the onset of difficult emotions are all examples of things that can cause our saboteurs to pipe up. Even though what they have to say isn't exactly encouraging, following them will give you a sense of control again. Remember, saboteurs are only concerned with keeping everything the same. So when you listen to them, they're happy. All is right in the world.

Saboteurs didn't always exist to trip you up, however. They originated when you were little to protect you. When you were young, you probably experienced something that, for a child your age, was potentially life-threatening. It could be a traumatic event, but it really doesn't have to be. If a parent doesn't pay enough attention to you one day, for example, as a small child you'll start to feel unloved. And if you're unloved as a toddler or baby who is dependent on her parent for survival, that signals a legitimate threat to your life. Your saboteurs jumped in and told you things like, *Smile even though you're unhappy,* or, *You're not cute enough*, and we quickly responded to correct the situation, smiling and behaving cutely.

Back then, they were your friend. They really did help you make sense of your world by telling you how to act. They helped you get love and attention, among other primary needs, and gave you a healthy fear of danger. They probably saved your life at one point or another.

Now that you're an adult, you have an incredible capacity to adapt, grow, and change, all while staying safe and even thriving. Your saboteurs, on the other hand, haven't evolved at all. They still have the very same concerns and beliefs about you that they had when you were little. They want you safe, at all costs, even if that cost is deep unhappiness.

As an adult, saboteurs will in fact save your life if you are in a truly life-or-death situation. They'll reduce reality to black-and-white, overlook nuances, and bypass complex thinking to speed up your decision-making. When your life is in danger, your saboteurs will step in, telling you what to do to reach safety and stay alive. Saboteurs speak the language of fear, and fear is your alert system. But most of the time, your life isn't in danger, and yet your saboteurs don't know that. All they know is fear and danger.

To a saboteur, any change means risk, and any risk means a threat to your life. Anytime you try to believe something is possible that you haven't validated by direct experience before (or even if you have), saboteurs will interpret that possibility or change as a threat to your life. They'll do their best to stop you.

When you're feeling uncertain, it's natural to want to be real with yourself; nobody wants to be deluded, so of course you're going to give these opinions a fair shake. You're a responsible person, and you want to make the smartest decision possible.

But if you accidentally put your saboteur in charge, you'll believe the smartest decision is to heed their warnings. If you trust the logic of your saboteurs, you'll end up believing that what you want isn't possible. Your brain will seek out evidence of this, to validate your decision, and it will find it. It will also filter out information that doesn't align with this point of view. Every time there's an opportunity to do something that will open a new door for yourself, even in the smallest of ways, you'll either be oblivious to it and miss it entirely, or you'll dismiss it, telling yourself on some level that it's not a good idea. You'll do this all while convinced that your logic is true and right. It's an innocent mistake, but one that tends to make us unhappy and unfulfilled over time.

What Happened When Alex Saw Through His Saboteurs

I have a client who made major breakthroughs in the first three months of coaching just by seeing his saboteurs. Alex came to me because, like you, he was stuck in a job he hated. He was a lawyer with passionate, activist interests, yet his job amounted to pushing paper. He didn't feel he was living his potential, and experienced disappointment about this on a daily basis. Yet he had no idea where to begin to create what he truly wanted. He was so miserable that his wife, who heard about my services, urged him to call me.

When Alex first came to me and told me about his job situation, he felt powerless to change anything. His dream of being an activist and making a real difference for immigrants and the people of his home country seemed so impossible and felt so weighty and mired in struggle that he told himself, *Oh, I shouldn't bother.* He thought the same kinds of things we all think when we have a dream like this: *I shouldn't be irresponsible. This is just a fantasy.* Now, he laughs in amazement when he remembers what he used to tell himself.

Alex experienced clarity quickly, at around month three. He investigated his thinking, and started to see it more objectively. He also learned to trust his ideas for his future, long enough to talk them through in our sessions. Soon he saw that his ideas weren't silly or based in fantasy. They were real and realistic. As he connected with his dream more and more, he took action. He planned his departure from his current company and how he would communicate this to his boss and co-workers. Then, he started his own practice as a lawyer, helping immigrants achieve asylum and citizenship. Through the work we did together, he learned how to trust his strengths and work from his strongest, most confident (and visionary) self, and two years later he started an NGO to protect immigrants and advance the cause of the people of his home country. Now (three years later), he is a leading expert who is invited to speak to Congress and the United Nations, so that our world leaders are better equipped to create peace in his home country and protect his people. Needless to say, Alex is doing work that matters to him, and he is making a true difference in the world. His work will potentially save thousands of lives.

Think about where the people of his home country and hundreds of immigrants in the U.S. would be if Alex had continued to trust his saboteurs! I bet you can imagine the impact on his wellbeing and self-respect, had he chosen to stay in a job that made him miserable because his saboteurs told him he shouldn't bother.

This is why I want to show you the difference between self-talk that seems trustworthy but can't be trusted, and self-talk that can be relied upon. If something you want is possible, the first step is to be able to *see* that it's possible. The next is to *believe* that it's possible. Then you take action and know you're moving in the right direction, even if it makes you feel vulnerable or unsettled.

How to Determine Which Inner Voice You Can Trust

Saboteurs have different ways of showing up, so it's important to be aware of how to spot them. When you feel powerless, for example, there's a saboteur on board. Saboteurs will tell you things like: *You don't have any power in this situation, You've been done wrong*, or *It's all his fault.* They'll often show up as blame. Blame keeps us powerless, and saboteurs like that, because even though powerlessness is painful, it keeps the status-quo going strong and prevents you from being able to create any changes. You can spot blame happening when you're railing against someone else, feeling self-righteous, or when you're reeling against yourself with anger and frustration.

Saboteurs can also say things like *It's not the right time*, or *It doesn't matter if I don't succeed*, or even *I don't care what happens*. They have sneaky, subtle ways of getting you to avoid or put off taking actions that will rock the boat. When you find yourself postponing something more than a couple times, yet the action is important to you, it's time to develop a strategy to move through your fear.

You can spot the presence of a saboteur even if you don't notice what they're communicating. The energy of saboteurs is heavy and serious, and no matter what actions you take, there's a feeling of struggle. If you observe closely, you'll notice that when you're under the influence of a saboteur, you'll feel constricted. You may feel tightness in your heart, tension in your shoulders, or a wrinkle forming between your eyebrows. Life will seem extra hard from this place. If you've spent enough time being run by your saboteurs, you can be convinced that all change is excruciatingly hard – or that the changes you want will require grueling work, when that's not necessarily true. Or at least, it doesn't have to be.

Another telltale sign that you've got a saboteur driving you is negative forecasting. Two words that tip me off to my client's saboteurs (and to my own when I hear them come out of my mouth) are "What if?" When you feel yourself shying away from action or commitment because you're wondering, *What if something goes wrong? What if I fail? What if I go blank when I get on stage?* you know it's time to stop and investigate your fears. "What if" questions are natural cues that can help you become well-prepared, but when they reduce your ability to handle a situation rather than improve it, that's when you know you're in saboteur territory.

And the last giveaway that your saboteurs are running the show is indecision. When you can't make a decision – whether it's a life-changing one or a simple one – and instead you keep spinning in circles, weighing one possible outcome against another, then you're in the grip of a saboteur. Saboteurs live in our heads (as opposed to our hearts), and when we experience something that scares us, a little or a lot, into our heads we go. This prevents us from experiencing pain in some ways, but it also leaves us with no grounding with which to prioritize and make real decisions. If your tasks pile up at work, but your productivity plummets because you can't prioritize, it's time to stop and lift yourself out of fear mode.

When you're listening to your true self, you won't have these experiences. You'll feel grounded and clear, with much less worry about the future. You may feel nervous and excited about a risk you're about to take, and you may feel vulnerable, but you'll have the sense that you're opening instead of constricting. You'll feel strong, and have access to your natural strengths. Everything will flow more easily, and actions won't feel laden with struggle. When you're operating from your true self, you don't get paralyzed by fear, blame, avoidance, or doubt because you'll be focused on what's possible and what's valuable to you, what you appreciate and what you're capable of.

Everything changes when you shift out of the saboteur's perspective and look at things through the lens of your true self. Your thoughts will change, your perceptions will change, and your experience will change. Saboteurs mean well, and it's best to approach those parts of yourself with compassion. But ultimately, if you want to live into your potential and challenge our own status quo by saying, *I believe it's possible to find work where I can make a difference*, you'll want to practice ignoring saboteur voices within you. It's time to replace that way of thinking with one that will be your ally instead of your nemesis.

Everything this book will cover from here will help you steer clear of saboteur thinking, because it will ground you in your natural strengths and gifts. But for now, simply work on spotting your saboteurs and ignoring them.

Take Action: Start Spotting Your Saboteur Voices

Based on what this chapter has brought up for you, expand your awareness of your own saboteurs. Consider: How do saboteurs show up in your life? What kinds of things do they say when you're about to challenge your own status quo, or dream big for yourself? (Examples: *Who do you think you are? You're unqualified for that. You're not good enough. You're not ready. Other people get to have what they want, but you don't – you're different.*) Write down every saboteur phrase you can think of, that shows up for you when you're about to do something new or scary and causes you to feel vulnerable.

Next, look at when you hear these voices or make decisions based on them. What impact have they had on you? How does listening to your saboteurs affect your energy or mood? How does it affect your confidence? How does it affect your willingness? Write down all the emotions, reactions, or experiences that happen in response to your saboteurs.

When you do listen to your saboteurs, what impact does it have on your actions? What ideas of yours have you postponed or dismissed altogether? How has this contributed to your current vision of your future? What are you seeing now about your saboteurs' effects on yourself or your life that you didn't see before? Take notes on everything you notice. The more observations you can make, the better.

Remember, everyone has these voices! Be kind to yourself as you discover how yours have influenced you. Celebrate your new awareness! Awareness is the first and most powerful step in creating new choices for yourself.

Pulling It All Together: Make Way for Possibility by Watching Your Self-Talk

Now that you know how to identify your saboteurs, and you understand the impact of listening to them, make a commitment to acknowledge their real intentions. They are there to keep things the same; when you're pressing on the gas to make your life change, they will step on the brakes. There's no need to give them power, especially if listening to them makes everything feel heavy and difficult.

Pay attention to the way your thinking makes you feel. Some thinking will pull you down, and some thinking will make you feel energized and engaged. Make sure you follow feelings of increased energy and engagement, for they indicate something positive is happening inside you. Whenever you're in the unknown because you're embarking on a change or thrown into a new situation, following the positive resonance inside you is a good rule of thumb. Even better, draw awareness from these feelings: What do they tell about what you value? What do they tell you about your natural abilities? What do they tell you about what you love to do? Begin to give the positive, creative ideas and feelings inside you more and more air time, and you'll learn to trust them and see where they take you.

CHAPTER
4

Take Charge of Your Reality with the Skill of Dreaming

Now that you've learned to identify your saboteurs so you can choose to ignore them, we have more room to look at what's possible for you. In this chapter, you'll focus on dreaming, seeing, clarifying, and knowing what it is you want. I find that most people don't have a crystal clear vision of what they want, let alone believe it's possible, because their saboteurs have been shutting the process down too early for clarity to form. I also find that once my clients have clarified what they want, and can see it and feel it, it starts to make sense as a valid idea. It no longer seems like a fantasy or distraction from reality. Their saboteurs slowly step back, which allows the real-life possibility of what they want to become apparent to them. This is where things get exciting!

But dreaming can be harder than it sounds. Dreaming that involves sincerity (because it comes with an intention to commit) is daring. It takes courage. It makes us vulnerable because we're allowing ourselves to want what we want, without any justifying.

Dreaming – even if we do it only for a moment – invites us to assume that we are worthy of experiencing what we long for. In order to envision the future we want, even though it happens only in our mind's eye, we also have to trust on some level that what we want is valid. Dreaming is inherently creative, and so it involves the same set of skills and attitudes required for the creative process. When you get good at dreaming, you empower yourself with the capacity to create. And what I want for you, more than anything, is for you to know that you can create what you want – at work, at home, in your relationships, in life in general. Creating is at the heart of leadership.

Why You Should Never Skip Over the Step of Dreaming

I've always identified myself as an artist, and when I tell people that, at least half the time people will respond with a statement about themselves like "Oh, I'm not creative," or, "I can't even draw a straight line." After years of these conversations, I've realized just how many (way too many!) people believe they aren't creative because as a kid in art class, their teacher (or some other authority figure) made them feel like they "couldn't do art." Any artist knows that when it comes to kids making art, this is nonsense. Most artists admire children's instincts and natural abandon when it comes to creating things.

If you've grown up with the idea that you can't create, you're not alone. I'd wager that the impact of this idea is that you've learned not to completely trust your own dreams and desires. Because of this, somewhere down the line you may have outsourced your dreams to a third party. You handed over your authority on what's possible and what's good – or what's worthy of your effort – to someone else like your boss, your spouse, your parents, or your friends, but have a hard time taking a stand for what *you* want. And if you're like me and so many others, when what you want isn't offered to you by the people you've given that power to, you get frustrated, and feel powerless and angry.

Here's the thing. There's a lot of general support out there for "following your dreams," but when it comes to pitching a real idea to someone around you who can't yet see your vision, or who has their own self-created limits on what is possible, that adage quickly gets pushed aside for an explanation of why it isn't possible. I believe most people give up on their dreams far too early because they decide what isn't possible long before they ask the question, *Under what circumstances would it be possible?* And maybe that's what you've also done without realizing it.

It's understandable, because this stage of the creative process – the visionary stage – involves great vulnerability. And even though vulnerability is a sign that we're truly invested, that we care, that we're willing, and that we are growing, we're not brought up to see it this way. Most of us experience it as a red flag – a sign of danger or that something's wrong – and out of fear, we shut our creative process down.

Sooner or later, we just forget that we can dream in the first place. While you can't wait to leave your job and would do anything to find a way out, and while you know you want to do work that makes a difference in this world, and while you know you want to be happy, you're probably so overwhelmed and stressed that your saboteurs are at the wheel, putting up roadblocks at every turn, because such change involves creative vulnerability.

Today, we're going to change that; I'm going to make you into the world's biggest cheerleader for dreaming. *Because you have a dream.* That's why you're reading this book. You've struggled to make it reality until now, but today you are officially turning over a new leaf. Today you take back your power. You decide what's real and what's not real – what's possible and what's not possible for you. Today you get to reconnect with the part of you who has just been waiting for airtime – the part of you who knows there's more for you.

Dreaming Will Open the Possibilities You've Been Longing For

Whatever dream you have, it will feel more like a fantasy and less like a real possibility when you're unclear. There's coming up with a dream, and there's *experiencing* the dream. Coming up with the dream looks like this: "I want to get out of this job and find work that's meaningful to me and makes a difference." (Notice the feeling of struggle inherent in that statement.) *Dreaming the dream* means taking time to envision – really see and feel – what you want. Dreaming means getting into your heart and asking it what it wants for you. Dreaming means experiencing *what it will be like* to have work that's meaningful to you, and seeing elements of what's involved in that work. Dreaming is connecting with the longing inside you and saying: *Talk to me. Tell me everything.* Dreaming is allowing yourself to come clean to yourself about what you don't like about your job (or your life) now, and why. Dreaming is patiently articulating to yourself what would be better, and how. Dreaming means allowing yourself to enjoy your version of how you want things to go, as you play it out in your mind's eye. When you spend time in the dreaming process, imagining what you want and looking inward at what you value and what brings you joy, you get to know yourself better. And when you know yourself better, clarity and confidence follow. Whenever we get closer to the truth of who we are, we feel stronger.

Whenever I feel ungrounded, or like things are moving too fast and I'm getting overwhelmed, I make sure to make time to dream. I sit on my couch in the morning with my tea, and I reflect on what I really want. *How do I want this week to go? How do I want to show up in this program I'm in? What outcomes do I want to create from this project?* When I'm clear, I know what to do. Dreaming really is the beginning stage of any creative process.

When dreaming, make sure you give yourself full permission to want *whatever* you want. Don't edit. And don't look to your head for answers, because it's too easy to get input based on what you "should" want, or what is your best guess of what would make you happy, rather than the truth. A more reliable source for information about what you want is your heart and your body. Close your eyes and get curious. Ask your heart a question. Listen for what shows up. A good rule of thumb is to make every answer okay. If what you get first is a wordless feeling of what you want, great! Work with that and build on it. Stay in that feeling until more information surfaces. If what comes up is an image, but you don't know what that image means, get curious: What's important about this? What do I like about this? What does this remind me of? Absolutely everything your intuition will give you is material with which you can get clear on what you really want.

Dreaming helps you do the work of building and clarifying. It's the most productive part of starting anything, and it's very different from fantasy. When you build a dream in your mind's eye, you're changing as a person while you do it. You're becoming the person who realizes this dream.

Dreaming Is a Way to Ensure Positive Future Experiences

Dreaming is the most important step in creating any change – including trying to figure out where you belong professionally – so you can make a difference. We can't skip this step. When we do, we only go in circles. In fact, if you're not accustomed to dreaming on a daily basis – if you haven't incorporated some intention into your actions, projects, hopes, and dreams – you may find yourself in what leadership expert Bob Anderson calls "reaction mode" much of the time. Reaction mode is what causes us to feel endlessly behind in our work: overwhelmed and resentful of the people making decisions that affect us, and constantly disappointed in our inability to move forward. Reaction mode keeps our wellbeing and productivity subject to the whims of everyone around us. Reaction mode keeps our focus on what's wrong and how much it bothers us. Reaction mode can make anything we do harder than it needs to be and far less enjoyable.

Consider this example of how you might plan an event for your company when in this mode:

You suddenly remember you've got to plan this party, and the timing's bad. This could be the task that puts you over the edge. So you buckle down and jump into the process, thinking, The sooner I start the better. *You find the date. You shop for invitations. You roll your eyes at the cost. You check your phone as you realize you're taking time away from more important projects. You try to make the process quick, but inevitably there's an endless stream of emails and phone calls to work out the details of coordinating caterer, event site, and music. Some days you work through lunch to catch up. Or you forget to eat. When the event comes, you put on a dress and a smile, and you get through it. You may succeed, and your guests may leave impressed, but the ultimate impact on you is exhaustion. And maybe even a little resentment. But hey, you survived.*

Compare this with the way dreaming gets us into creation mode. Creation mode, as Anderson explains in his white paper *Mastering Leadership*, leads us to an entirely different place. Creation mode keeps us engaged and empowers us to shift things in a positive direction. When we're in creation mode, we're conscious of the outcomes we want, and we're always seeking to create them. As an example, take a look at how this party planning situation might look different in creation mode:

When you remember you have to plan this party, you sit down with a blank sheet of paper and start to dream up ideas of what you want, and take notes. Your first task is deciding what you want to create. You take the timing of this into consideration: One key outcome you want is limited stress put on you. You dream of an easy party to put on that makes everyone feel great. You realize you could use a mood boost, since it was a long winter, so you want the feel of the party to be bright, light, and gregarious.

Since you know it will be more fun – and easier – to do this with others, you immediately call a creative friend to help brainstorm. You and she talk, and the two of you laugh as you consider some pretty outrageous ideas. You settle on a couple components that will create joy: salsa dancing, and a dance instructor to lead some fun exercises. It's a bit out of the box, but you go with it. You can't help but talk about your fun idea over lunch with colleagues, and they naturally offer some resources. You take everyone up on every offer, knowing that the more help you'll have, the less stress there will be on you.

Suddenly, you've got the music booked, the venue reserved, and already a good portion of your guests are getting ready to ham it up come party time. You have a team of co- creators making this event a hit, and you're feeling really fulfilled by how fun the process is…

And the outcome of the party? Just the emotional uplift you needed, and a bright, light, gregarious mood for your guests.

When we start by dreaming, we lay an expectation of enjoyment and build on it. We start by getting clear on what we want, and enjoy a little imaginative reverie before we even take action. When in reaction mode, we're always a victim; it seems that we're powerless to create anything good. But when in creation mode, we're clear about the outcome we want, which positions us perfectly to see how we might get there.

You can stop for a moment to dream up your ideal outcome before doing just about anything. You can dream up how you want to feel at the end of your subway commute (rested and grounded), and then come up with a couple strategies that might get you there (listening to a meditation app and being mindful the whole way or spending your time reflecting on what you love most about your kids). You can dream up how you want your next quarterly review to go and consider how you might facilitate that outcome.

When it comes to the task at hand – finding work you love where you can make a difference – you can certainly dream up your ideal outcome for that. Even if you don't know all the details yet, you can spend time in dream-mode, imagining what you know that you want. What will it feel like to make a difference? What expression do you see on your face? How will you enjoy the people around you? How will you feel when you come home from work each day? Don't worry if your vision doesn't appear in totality right now. You'll build on it.

Use Dreaming as a Way to Stay Empowered

Because the habit of dreaming keeps you in creation mode, it also prepares you for taking action. Dreaming puts you in a place of positivity, because you're only thinking about outcomes that would satisfy you and bring you enjoyment. This helps you stay in touch with all the positive emotions associated with your dream, like hope, excitement, care, and fulfillment. When you're grounded in all the good that can come of taking the next step, you're more likely to take it. Also, when you're resonating with all this goodness and positive feeling (which essentially comes from love), fear tends to fade away and become a non-issue. So, what becomes of all those fears that grip you and keep you utterly convinced that you don't know what you want, you don't know how to move forward, or that you don't have what it takes? They melt away. They're just not as absolute as they make themselves out to be. Yay for that!

When you stay tuned into all the positive emotions that come with imagining your desired future, you also feed and expand a different part of you: not the same as when you only mull over your obstacles. Dreaming is like fertilizer for the part of you who is ready, strong, capable, lovable, excited, and alive. The more you welcome this part of yourself and spend time listening to her, the more she will come out for you. And the energy she brings will be infectious. It's like magic.

Even though you know you want to find meaningful work – and at this point you must in order to preserve your sanity – you may have no idea what that meaningful work is, or how to get it. That's okay. Making a habit of feeding the part of you who is just aching to come out and play will ignite a change inside you. You'll feel stronger and more confident and more ready to take action.

Use Dreaming to Help You Brave the Unknown

You know, the barriers you feel are real. You're not messed up, and your boss doesn't really rule your destiny – and yet, the change you want requires enormous courage. Why? Because your decision to get yourself unstuck, to change your mindset, and dare to imagine something totally new for yourself is a total disruption to your own status quo. It's likely a disruption to the status quo around you, too. You may be thinking in ways or wanting things for yourself that your family never has. You may be looking at the big picture – seeing possibilities that your boss and coworkers can't see, at least not yet. You may be wanting something that seems impossible for you, and yet, you still want it.

Challenging our status quo is truly frightening at times. You just don't know what will happen, and it's easy to conjure up horror movies in your head about the future. You're challenging your basic brain framework – laying down entirely new brain pathways and belief systems. You're using your prefrontal cortex to override what's primal and automatic for you. If you're an adventurous type like me, this can sound exciting. But how do you know you'll be okay?

Dreaming and envisioning positive outcomes (and resonating in all those positive emotions that come along with it) will help calm your nervous system and reassure you that you're safe. It helps you stay clear about where you're headed, and it grounds you in hope and expectation. When you actively dream about what you want to create, you support yourself in the unknown by having a clear direction. This frees you to focus on what you want to do next, rather than feeling as though something is about to happen to you. With this level of calm and focus, you can see your progress and reassure yourself in real-time that you're doing the right thing (and course-correct if you aren't). Connecting with your dreams on a continual basis helps you keep marching forward in the throes of the unknown, like a clear, strong leader.

Create a Safe Place for Your Dreamer to Emerge

Actively dreaming takes courage and will. You have the skills you need to dream, yet they may not be the ones you're used to highlighting, so I'm going to walk you through them here. They're basic and human – everyone has them – yet stepping into them is a bit of an art form.

Appreciate Your Vulnerability and Innocence

Dreaming takes vulnerability and innocence. When you were a kid, using your imagination in this way came easily to you. But as an adult, this may not be the case. You may feel goofy, letting yourself enjoy thinking about something you want when you don't even know if it's possible yet. Part of you may not want to risk looking like a fool – or worse, appearing arrogant. That worry is a result of your natural vulnerability, which is what we feel when our heart's invested. It's a sign we care. You're not naive to dream. You're brave.

Feeling vulnerable and wobbly indicates you're giving yourself room to grow and play in a way you haven't before. It means you're expanding and relating to your creative self with respect and honor. It's also a sign that you're starting to trust yourself.

So go ahead, feel foolish, feel goofy, feel vulnerable … feel like a kid. That part of you who feels like a kid just might be the part who has the answer to all of your questions. She may be the one who knows exactly what would bring you joy, how that would make life different for you, and what you should do next.

Trust Your Intuition

If you were a student in my art class, with some paper and drawing supplies, trying to draw from your imagination, I wouldn't stand over you with a stick, pressuring you to make something up on the spot. I'd probably make sure there's some nice music on. I'd make sure there was something for me to do like open and close windows, or gently fuss with supplies, but I'd be waiting patiently, trying to be a loving presence for your creative self to feel safe and invited. I'd be holding space for something to come out of you, in just the way that it wants.

That's how I want this to go for you. You don't have to push any visions out of yourself, and you don't have to force clarity. Be the loving adult in the background, holding space for something to appear. And when it does appear, go with it. Don't judge. Just be curious. Notice the impact on you: Does it feel good? Does it make you feel lighter? Are you enjoying yourself? The key is to follow your nose, and let it lead you deeper and deeper into feelings of love, satisfaction, joy, and fulfillment.

I've had clients who were convinced they didn't know what they wanted, or even holding to the lie that they were "incapable of visioning." But that never turned out to be the case. Your answers, your clarity, your wisdom really are already inside you. All you need to do is practice listening.

Be Open to Receiving

When you dream about what you want, you're putting yourself in the position of receiving what you want and enjoying it.

It's important to be in receiving mode, so that when your change happens in real life, you're open to it. I want you to be able to see your vision of the future clearly, and feel what it feels like to get it. I'd love for you to be able to observe your experience of this closely. If you can identify these sensations and emotions while you experience them, then you know that the dream is alive in you.

It takes love to do this. You have to love yourself and, for a moment, be willing to receive everything you want within your mind's eye. It never ceases to amaze me how capable we are of giving ourselves the experiences we need (more about this in the Healing chapter). When you do receive, bask in it! Take all the time you need. Come back to it as often as you can. Start to experience the joy, satisfaction, and fun of knowing exactly what you want to do in life, making the difference you want to make. Prime your system for the experiences coming your way, so that when your life changes, adjusting will be easy.

How Robyn's Dream for Her Future Surprised Her

If you find the blank slate of dreaming up what you want too intimidating, this story is for you. I had one client, Robyn, who told me at the beginning of a session that she had no idea what she really wanted to do with her life. This client is young, in a fine job, but was coaching with me to make sure she pointed herself in the right direction as she made career decisions. She was convinced that she couldn't come up with the answer to her question of *What's my purpose?* and *What kind of meaningful work do I want?* But 30 minutes into the session, she'd found it already.

How did she get there so quickly? I asked her "What drives you crazy – like, what do you sometimes witness in the world that you just can't tolerate?" She told me that whenever she sees a homeless kid on the street or a young person living out of their car, for the next hour or more, she hears questions in her head like: *How does that kid get a job if they don't have an address? What do they write on their application?* and *If they do get a job, how do they receive paychecks in the mail, or mail in general?* and *Do they have a phone? How do they pay for it? How do they get a bank account without an address?* These questions run on and on and on within her.

When she told me this, I said, "Robyn, you know, most people who come across a kid living in their car would just feel bad and walk away." This really told me everything about her – what she cared about, what got her energized, and it even clued me into what she wanted. We continued, this time with me guiding her into dream mode. She envisioned what she'd rather see, rather than this situation of kids living in cars and struggling. She wanted to be able to do something about that. She wanted to protect those kids. She wanted to advocate for them.

She imagined what that would be like, and who she would get to be in that role. She imagined the skills that would show up, and how she might grow as a leader. She saw what she'd be wearing and what her desk would look like. She imagined how efficient and committed she would be. Suddenly she was filled with feelings of fulfillment. I could practically feel her glow through the phone. This is what she'd been wanting. Her job was fine, but it wasn't this.

This was her dream.

Notice, the important part of Robyn's realization is that she felt her dream clearly and viscerally. She knew she was on the right track because of how her body, emotions, and outlook changed as she envisioned it. There's room to refine and develop the dream once it takes root in this way. The outcome you manifest will develop and shift, but because of your ability to dream, you will stay connected to that inner core inside you that knows your direction, knows what's good for you, and trusts that it is possible.

Take Action: Relax and Connect with Your Dream

Now it's time for you to connect with what you long for by dreaming. Before you get started, it's helpful to sit quietly for a moment, to make sure you're in a more relaxed state. Breathing into your heart and focusing your attention there will help you settle and get your intuition on board.

The first thing I want you to explore is: *What dream do you know you have, but feel too silly to say out loud?*

No matter how outlandish or even immature this dream may seem, it's your starting place. Stay there and imagine it fully. Sit with each of these questions: *What would you love about getting this dream to happen? What's important about that? What would it feel like to be there? Who would you get to be? How would you change? How would your life change?*

There's so much information in this cast-away dream of yours, and that's what you're exploring here. It could be that in the future, you end up getting exactly what you want as it appears in this dream. But it could also be that you learn so much more from the exploration, that your desired (dreamed-of) outcome changes. For example, when I was little I wanted to be an artist and a business person. I'd say that I'm living that dream now, because the feeling of that dream is the same: I get to create experiences and products, and I run my own business. But I call myself a coach. There are many ways to live out our dreams, and the right way for you will emerge.

So give yourself full permission, and keep listening for and feeling into the essence of what you want, rather than the exact title or label. Enjoy what you create in your mind's eye!

Pulling It All Together: Take Charge of Your Reality with the Skill of Dreaming

Dreaming is the first step in creating any change, and it will position you to create what you want, no matter what situation you're in. It's a way to calm your nervous system, energize yourself with positive emotions, and help you clarify your future. If you make dreaming a habit, you'll find yourself less stressed out, less overwhelmed, and more empowered. You'll build comfort in the unknown and become a strong decision maker at work and in your personal life.

As you use dreaming to center yourself more and more, you'll notice you'll feel more optimistic about the future. Things you wanted that once felt out of reach will slowly appear reasonable and likely. As you witness yourself creating the outcomes you want, you'll build credibility and trust in yourself. Add that to all the positive emotions you'll be feeling, and you'll feel a whole new sense of freedom.

My wish for you is to tap into this deep well of wisdom that's within you, and lean into it every day. I'd love for you to empower yourself to create the exact experiences you want to have, including the opportunity to do work that's meaningful to you.

Embrace the Game- Changing Act of Commitment

Concerning all acts of initiative and creation, there is
one elementary truth the ignorance of which kills count-
less ideas and splendid
plans: that the moment one definitely commits oneself,
then providence moves too.

–Johann Wolfgang von Goethe

After spending nearly a decade experiencing and witnessing transformational change in myself and others, I've come to see that, when you really need a big change, yet you know you have your own fears, habits, and patterns to face, a compelling commitment is what you need to get there.

Every life-changing transformation I've been through involved the same thing. Stakes were high, and I was forced to decide for myself that I would get what I wanted in the end. This didn't mean I expected to be given the outcome I was seeking, or that I expected a safe way around the obstacles that separated my goal and me. It meant I was aware that it was up to me to create lemonade out of lemons, and even though it scared me like hell to do it, I had to commit to trying.

This happened when I found myself in a life crisis that turned out to be an incredibly positive and life-changing experience. It also happened when I signed up for a year-long experiential leadership program, the idea of which scared the crap out of me but gave me everything I wanted. And it's happened with every major commitment I've found myself making that has intimidated me, from leading workshops, to public speaking, to writing this book. In all cases, I was out of my comfort zone. I knew well the barriers that had stopped me in the past (like fear, lack of experience, and my saboteur stories), and I had no guarantee of any positive outcome. There was nothing safe about any of these commitments, and I could have chosen to create fear-based stories from them, by looking at everything that could go wrong.

Yet with each of these experiences, things went exactly as I hoped. In each, there was something I deeply wanted – the ability to overcome fear of public speaking, or an ability to connect more fearlessly and intimately with strangers as a coach, or deeper connection with my wisdom and strengths so that I could experience life and love with more confidence. The reason things went exactly as I'd hoped is that I had a clear choice to make, inside a high-stakes commitment. I could choose to create to avoid what I feared, or I could try to create what I wanted. In each I chose to decide that it was already foretold that I would get what I wanted. I just had to summon the courage to live it. I decided I would do my best to create what I wanted within each circumstance, no matter the discomfort I experienced and no matter how much it looked like things could go south.

This kind of decision is a state of mind you can choose to be in. You declare, "This is so," and then you live it, making every decision in favor of possibility, no matter how vulnerable you feel. It's a state of mind, and it's a way of seeing things. In any circumstance, you can perceive all the internal and external barriers working against you and use that to add up to a foretold negative conclusion, or you can assume that the opposite is true: that all perceived internal and external barriers are working for you, bringing you exactly what you need to grow into the person you need to be to reach this goal.

Commitment is a state of mind, and it's also a powerful structure. It involves a concrete goal, an endpoint or objective that you try to achieve to within a time frame, and it often happens within constraints. Think of structures like getting your doctorate degree, or writing a book, or creating a website, or outdoor leadership trips, or other professionally-led programs.

In this chapter, I'll show you how to use commitment as a structure to get what you want, both from yourself and for yourself. The magic and miracles you dream of will happen when you commit to your soul's longing and your heart's wisdom, and decide that *This will be*.

Give Yourself Permission to Create Your Own Opportunities

You Don't Need to Believe in Made-Up Limitations

When you're trying to create a change that requires you to grow as a person, normal problem-solving and goal-setting isn't always enough to take you there. It's totally normal to try these methods, and watch yourself fail, and then become disappointed, and then disillusioned over time. When this happens, it's not a signal to stop trying. It is an announcement that what you're actually being called into is a hero's journey or transformation. You are on the cusp of a deep and magical change, one that your intellect cannot predict or even understand.

But if you don't see this, you won't see opportunities to take a leap into that change. Big commitments are scary, and when you're feeling disempowered and stuck, you're likely to dismiss them as unreasonable or impossible. This is only because you've developed a skewed understanding of your limits. There have been so many things I was convinced I couldn't do, because of a story I made up about myself, that when I did them I looked back and thought, *I can't believe I was so convinced I couldn't do that.*

When you spend years, even decades, inside the same thought patterns, unconsciously believing made-up stories about who you are, you start to paint that reality as "real." You trust it more than any other. But once you see this, and look at your made-up limitations with a healthy dose of skepticism, you can start to move beyond them.

You Don't Need to Wait for External Validation

We live in an age where everything can be backed up with data. We test ideas before we run them and scientifically prove outcomes before getting invested. We constantly seek external, consensus-based validation for what we believe and how we see the world. If you're in an environment where everyone around you believes that starting your own non-profit is too hard and you can't make money that way, or if everyone believes you're good at project management so you can't also be good at art or healing, then you may start to believe that too.

Using commitment as a structure to launch you into exponential growth does the opposite. When you use commitment this way, you run on trust, wisdom, willingness, and creativity. You don't wait to prove anything. Instead, you commit, and in the process, you redefine what is real and what is possible for yourself. It's the ultimate training in trusting yourself and building confidence.

You Don't Need to Wait Until Conditions Are Right

If you're stuck in an office job that bores you, it's normal to want your circumstances to change, but beware of the trap of waiting until conditions are right. You may think you need the support, and you may think you need external confirmation that you're not crazy for wanting a career change. That may be true, but if you're not getting those things now from your current thinking and environment, sadly it doesn't mean you'll get them later. If you keep waiting for things to be different, you could wait indefinitely. How long are you willing to wait? Five years? Ten? Thirty?

It may be true that the conditions you're in now aren't right. But they may never be, especially if you're standing by, waiting for them to change. Although if *you* do the changing, you'll open new possibilities. It takes enormous courage to do this, but it's incredibly liberating when you realize you aren't beholden to the circumstances around you!

Why a Compelling Commitment Will Be Your Catalyst

With the kind of change you want – one that requires transformation – you'll encounter resistance, and so you'll need something more powerful than goal-setting to launch you forward. Commitment that requires you to stretch will allow you to surprise yourself. When you truly commit to creating an outcome before you know how you'll make it happen, you activate an entirely different set of inner resources than you do with mere goal-setting. You're asking yourself to create a miracle. You won't do that by only applying hard work and focus alone. Hard work and focus are what got you here. To move beyond this place, you'll have to trust and have faith in a much larger possibility.

Can you sense what changes for you when you move from a mindset of goal-setting to one of creating a miracle? Creating miracles requires trust and courage; they call us forth. When we truly commit to moving beyond fear to create something big, our whole being senses it, and we know we need to summon more than just our small selves. Suddenly, inner resources and strengths get mobilized that were previously latent, or asleep. Insights come and synchronicity happens. We get over our shyness at asking for help, and we ask. And when we get the help we need, we receive it.

Commitment moves you into the unknown on the basis of trust, willingness, and surrender. You may not understand how you'll be able to accomplish your goal of finding your true purpose and finding work that allows you to live it. But once you commit, you will start to see what it will take to get there, and your physical, emotional, and spiritual being will begin to rise to the occasion. Once you decide that something will be, then it will be. It's your resistance to change that stopped you before, yet after you surrender to truly welcoming it, magical change will begin.

A Game-Changing Commitment Will Call on the Best of You

You'll Need a Sincere Invitation of Self

Commitment like this won't work if it's done out of self-judgment, or a sense of rushing yourself, or out of a demand for progress. Those approaches are a way of fighting who you are. There's no need to fight yourself. Your dream of meaningful, joy-rendering work will take you further into who you are, and invite more of your natural gifts to surface. The essential challenge inherent in a commitment isn't to overcome something you aren't. It's to drop the thoughts and ideas that keep your limited self-image intact. It's to relinquish the stories, beliefs, and habits that are creating your stuckness, so that you can emerge more freely and more fully as yourself.

You'll want to approach your commitment with a sincere, trusting, open invitation to yourself. Meet yourself with as much love, compassion, and appreciation as you can muster. Be sure you're making this commitment from your heart.

You'll Need a Clear Vision

When you choose a structure like a compelling commitment to hold your change, you'll need a clear sense of where you're headed. You don't have to have all the details of the outcome in place, but you do have to start with some level of knowing. For example, when I entered the leadership program that changed my life, I knew what I wanted and needed to get out of the program. I had a visceral sense of where I was headed: I could feel it, sense it, and envision some of the details of what would be different for me if I got what I wanted out of it. As a highly sensitive person who feared speaking in front of groups, feared giving workshops, and wasn't living my potential (but wanted to make a difference), I knew that after this program I would be different. I would emerge with the strengths I knew on a gut level were already inside me. I'd harness them, begin to step into my purpose, and I'd also gather the kind of richly committed and fiercely real yet loving community I'd longed for.

You'll Have a Clear Choice of Creating a Positive Outcome

It was a quarter of my way through that year, in the midst of chaos and personal struggle, that I said to one of my course leaders: "I decided I'm going get everything I want from this program." He responded: "You're going to get everything you *need*." That's the thing. When you have a clear vision of where you want to go, and you courageously step offshore into the unknown with all the heart and commitment you can gather, the universe will respond by giving you what you need to get there. That doesn't mean it will look pretty or feel easy. In fact, your most uncomfortable moments – where you feel the greatest resistance – will be the ones that carry you over to the other side.

To make the most of your commitment, you must decide to fully participate in the process of creating what you want from your experiences. You must take everything that happens internally and externally, and be curious: *How is this happening for me and for the sake of my growth? What can I create with this experience, to bring myself closer to where I am headed? What is this moment here to teach me? What's the importance of what I'm learning or experiencing right now?*

These are all ways you can choose to create a positive outcome from everything that happens in your life in the midst of your compelling commitment.

If Confidence Is What You're Looking for, Make a Game-Changing Commitment

The best part of using commitment as a tool for change is the confidence you feel afterward. It's thrilling, first of all, to watch yourself do something you swore you couldn't just a few months before. It's freeing to know and see that your beliefs, which felt so fixed in truth to you before, were merely your perception, and your perception can always be changed. It helps you see that you're more malleable and much stronger than you thought you were. You can adapt. You show up for yourself. It builds credibility. If you struggle with trusting yourself in life, commitment is your way out of that struggle. You've got to test all of your beliefs (particularly the negative ones!) before you resign yourself to acting on them for the rest of your life.

Because you'll know your way around trusting yourself in the unknown, and you've met your monsters in the dark and turned the light on, you'll be able to trust in the hidden strength and courage of others too. Commitment requires that you look for every ounce of strength you have and resonate with it, focus on it, and build on it. You get to see the best in you, because your commitment asks for the best in you. And when you want to bring out the best in someone else, you'll know how to look for it and see it in them, too. You'll be able to be their champion.

The ultimate benefit is true confidence, as a coach of mine defined it: Confidence is knowing you can handle what comes your way. Confidence isn't knowing what will come your way, and it's not appearing to others to know what you're doing. It's recognizing that even when you don't know what you're doing, you're still fully capable of responding in the moment and moving forward. You're never disqualified. You keep yourself qualified by staying in the game. You can apply this to everything you do, for the rest of your life. Experiencing yourself rising to your own commitments will give you ninja-like adaptability.

What Happened the Moment Rich Surrendered to His Commitment

When a previous client, Rich, came to me, he'd failed several interviews. He hated his job, where his boss rejected every creative idea he had, and where he felt forced to lower his standards (and be okay with that). He wanted out, big time.

About three months into our one-on-one coaching, Rich got impatient. Shouldn't he just apply for more jobs? What were we doing sitting around and talking about all this stuff? I had to remind him that was exactly the strategy he'd used in the past, and it hadn't worked. I also had to help him see what was really happening. He wasn't just looking to change his job. He was changing the behaviors that were preventing him from getting a job. And once he changed them, they'd be changed for good, so he'd have lots of options in the future. He wouldn't be held back anymore.

Rich surrendered to the process, and with trust and humility, he committed fully to achieving his dream end-goal of finding meaningful work. Focusing on applying for jobs had inadvertently caused Rich to skip over the real heart of the matter. This strategy, because it was so externally focused, prevented him from changing as a person in the ways he was being called to. When he took a closer look, he found that he was showing up in ways that kept his biggest strengths hidden from others. He was operating from his inner saboteurs without knowing it, and this wasn't helping him.

After getting clear on his mission, his purpose, his values, and his best strengths, Rich changed how he showed up in life and in work. He kept his focus on what he was creating, what he wanted, and all the strengths he could offer in the service of creating that. He took it upon himself to act in all the ways he wished others around him were acting, just so he could respect himself and know he was doing good work.

After this turnaround in Rich's approach, he got recruited on LinkedIn for exactly the kind of job he was dreaming of – one where he'd get to improve processes using his management and innovation skills. He interviewed, made a great impression, got an offer, and took the job. Whenever I hear from Rich today, he always makes sure to tell me that he still practices getting into his best self every day, and that things are going great because of it.

Take Action: Find A Structure to Ground Your Next Commitment

To create a compelling commitment, settle into seeing and feeling the outcome you want, until it rings clear in your heart. Connect with your longing like you did in the dreaming chapter and envision your desired future. What is it that you know about where you are headed? What is your visceral feeling or body sense of what it would feel like to be there? What is clear about who you will be when you reach this goal? How will you show up differently in life? What kinds of things (or parts of you) will you have left behind? What new experiences will you now be open to?

Explore why you've chosen this outcome as your destination. What about this outcome pleases your soul? What makes it important to you?

Next, look for a structure that will help you invoke this vision of yours, by summoning your full commitment. What is the outcome you are committing to creating? Who or what will provide the space and support for your transformation? What limit or deadline will determine the timeline of your journey? How will you proclaim your commitment to others? What resources and supports will you lean into to keep moving forward?

Pulling It All Together: Embrace the Game-Changing Act of Commitment

If you know that getting unstuck and stepping into the future you long for will require great change and courage on your part, and if the thought of taking that leap scares you, try making a compelling commitment to your goal and sharing it with others. In this moment, you may feel as though your commitment has already started. You may know on some level that you have already started changing. In some small but significant ways, you're already becoming a different person, by acknowledging who you are and where you're headed, and by relinquishing self-limiting stories and perspectives that have kept you stuck.

If you're feeling this way, you don't need any more evidence that you'll succeed, you don't need to wait until you feel fully capable, and you don't need to wait for the right time. You will create your own success, and you will build your capacity along the way. State your commitment and start creating!

Step Two in Creating Change: Believe That You Are Capable of Achieving Your Dream

Congratulations! You have completed learning about the first skill in creating your transformation: *Believe that your dream is possible,* by discarding sabotaging thoughts, trusting yourself to envision what you want and embracing game-changing commitment. Now it's time to work the skill of Step 2: *Believe that you are capable of achieving your dream.*

Now that you know where you're headed and you're committed to getting there, we want to address your belief that you can do it. Believing you are capable of achieving your dream isn't about convincing yourself of anything, and it's not about affirmations. It's about taking a good, solid look at everything that makes you feel strong and confident, and knowing how to tap into that when you need it.

When I work with clients around highlighting what makes them truly unique, strong, and amazing, it often feels like magic. It's like someone just turned the lights on, and suddenly everything glitters. It feels great for me as coach to be witness to them, and it feels great for my clients to experience their power and depth of inner resources. What's so amazing about this is that these parts of us were there all along. We don't have to struggle to become someone we're not, we just have to become more of who we are, and trust that what we need is inside us.

In the next three chapters, you'll explore your strengths from three different angles and learn tools to carry you beyond what currently stops you from taking action. You'll have ways to practice shifting your focus so that you stay in your strongest self, prevent yourself from getting distracted, and recover more quickly from setback.

Use these tools in your arsenal not just to create the work experience you want for yourself, but to create anything you want for yourself.

Awaken to Your Purpose and Use It for Good

Behind everything you do, there is a "why." Whether you're aware of them or not, you're acting on underlying motivations. Those motivations are pointed at creating something – a specific outcome, experience, or feeling. You are always creating.

That's why it's so important and powerful to be conscious of what your purpose is. If you don't investigate your why and if you don't ask yourself what's important to you and what you want to create, then you'll create something unconsciously. Some other part of you will do the decision making. That part of you will provide the logic behind your thoughts and actions. In that case, you'll create what that part of you wants. But not all self-talk is created the same, remember? It's important to make sure you know who you're putting in charge.

In this chapter, we're going to talk about purpose, so that you can make certain that you create the life and work you truly want. For example, why do you want a career change at this point in time? What's important about that to you? Why try to change anything at all? There's something already driving you to read this book and create change. That's your purpose beginning to speak up. Many times, when we're asked about our purpose, the question is so big and encompassing that it can make us freeze. How are we supposed to know the answer to that question?! But the answer isn't something you need to make up, or struggle to find, or win from doing lots of hard work. Your purpose is inside you, waiting to be seen, heard, and followed. Your job is to garner the courage to trust it.

Awakening to your purpose is a quest worth wrestling with (it's not your purpose you'll wrestle with, but the doubts and fears that cover it up), because your purpose will reveal who you are. And that will have you approaching your life and your work from this place: you, bringing the value you already have, to co-create a positive impact. In other words, instead of hunting, striving, winning, competing for, getting, or earning your value as a person from someone or something outside you (which we often use work to do), you will stand in your innate value and ability to contribute. You will fully own your goodness as a human being, and the gifts and wisdom you have cultivated up until this point. This is another way of saying: You'll move from a paradigm of scarcity (*I don't have. I need to get. I wish I could but I can't.*) to a paradigm of abundance (*I have enough. I can create. I either choose not to, or I choose to do my best.*).

Being who you are is important for a lot of reasons, and I don't say that only to make you feel warm and fuzzy in this moment (although I'm all for warm and fuzzy). Being who you are can be revolutionary. It can change your life, and it can change others' lives, too. Why? For one, it's real. It takes courage and vulnerability to be real. When you decide to "just be yourself," you expose your humanity. You give up using all the tactics you thought you needed before to control how well you're perceived, treated, and loved. This means that, whatever you do, you're in it to contribute and do your best and make a difference.

It's also much easier to live from your purpose, because it takes a lot of energy to control how others feel about you and treat you. It takes even more energy to be proving yourself all the time, even if only to yourself. Living from who you are and your life's purpose takes a lot of the noise out of the way, lets you listen to (and for) what's important, and lets you show up to life clear and willing.

What you will put your energy into is having the courage to live this way. When you live from purpose, you do so from your heart. That will make you vulnerable. You'll be called to grow and change. Only a compelling purpose, one that comes from deep inside you, will keep drawing you forward.

Connecting with your purpose, which is already ready and waiting inside you, will help you find your path. Your purpose will guide you into the next chapter of your life where you feel fulfilled by meaningful work, and once you get there, it will sustain you. It will feed your motivation and energy, and it will also feed your soul.

Living Your Purpose Takes Guts, and Here's Why

It's Scary to Own Your Light

While it's a drag to feel like you're being held back, it's more comfortable than trusting your power to make a difference, because the belief that you're held back functions to protect you from change. Trusting your power feels vulnerable, and most of us have a complicated relationship with vulnerability. When you connect with your purpose and your gifts, and you realize you really are powerful – because you have the power to make a difference – it can be surprisingly scary.

I've always been a very empathetic and intuitive person. I remember when I first became a coach, back when I was a Professional Organizer, and I saw my power clearly for the first time. I could connect with people quickly, help them hear and understand their emotions and thinking, and I watched my impact on them. While I always focused on making a positive impact, I suddenly feared the possibility of making a negative impact. Did I know enough about what I was doing? Did I really trust myself? Once I realized I could use my powers for good (something I'd hungered for through years prior), my mind conjured up everything that could go wrong, too.

Owning your unique ability to make a positive impact requires not only that you own your light – and admit that there isn't anything stopping you from making a difference – but it also requires you to be willing to take responsibility for your journey and your impact. If you doubt yourself too much, or if you don't have the support to make it through this challenge, you might not take the risk.

It Makes Your Heart Visible

I've talked to so many people who experience a clean separation between the work they do for a living and the things they care deeply about, personally. It's as if anything that's deeply personal doesn't belong in the work context. If it's personal, it's inappropriate, goes the thinking. This is a function of our saboteurs. Creating this deep divide protects us from being hurt or challenged to the point of disruption. While this may seem like it creates a more efficient path, in the end it doesn't. Working without a personal sense of purpose is exhausting; it's exactly what makes work feel like work.

Wearing a mask at work will protect you from feeling hurt or taking anything personally, but that mask is also what's causing you to feel more and more distant and alienated. It's what makes you doubt yourself and run your mind in circles around the idea of a job change. It's what makes you frustrated with your boss, or your co-workers, or your partner for not "letting" you flourish.

The antidote is coming clean about who you are and what you really think and care about. It's letting yourself be seen. When you do this, you open yourself to judgment, or criticism, or challenges to what you believe, some or all of which you may take personally. That hurts. But this will also force you to question yourself in a way that results in a deeper, truer relationship with your purpose. It will help you grow.

We're Used to Being "Good," Not Being Real

When you're in your twenties and just starting to take your career seriously, you take cues from the adults around you, and you apply the logic you learned throughout your education to do well. At that stage, you may be more concerned with security than anything else. If that was your case, you probably developed a habit of making sound decisions based on the decisions you saw people making. You didn't have enough life experience to do otherwise.

Now, however, you know how to make sound decisions for yourself. You don't hunger for security as much as you hunger for the feeling of being alive and inspired. If you're like many of my clients, rather than security, you long to have more skin in the game. You want greater risk, if it means you get to be real.

Moving from a mindset of safety and security, or even one of success-at-all-costs, to a mindset of working from heart and making a difference requires a paradigm shift. Paradigm shifts are disruptive. They mean change. Big change! It's easy to want this and at the same time continually put it off and wait for "more clarity." No one is completely ready for a paradigm shift. The very nature of experiencing a shift this great means you're going to be deeply uncomfortable, as you let go of old beliefs and take the leap to trust new ways of seeing the world and yourself.

Awakening to Your Purpose Will Make Life Easier

Your Purpose Will Guide You

You're embarking on a big change. You want to leave your job, and not only that, but you're also taking the leap to find work that means something to you. You've set out to make a difference. How will you know what direction to go? How will you know it's right for you? How will you know if it's worth the risk involved? This journey requires being in the unknown, and most of us freak out when we're in the unknown. It's not an easy place to be.

Because you are setting out to do work that's truly right for you – not someone else – you will need to trust your knowing, rather than the logic of saboteurs or smaller selves. You'll need some experiential sense that where you're going will lead you where you want to go. Your purpose will do that for you.

Your purpose is something that resonates so truly and deeply inside you that when you're in touch with it, your fears will calm and your saboteur voices will mellow. You'll be in a perspective of serving and creating for the sake of something much bigger than you. That something will carry you forward, over and beyond where you think you can go. Because your purpose resonates directly with your heart, where your wisdom resides, it will give you the courage and comfort you need to endure the discomfort of change.

You'll Experience Greater Flexibility

Your job of finding meaningful work, of awakening to your life's purpose, is not a matter of getting the right "application." This means that it's not about finding the exact right job with the exact right title. Your purpose lives inside you. It's a function of your intention and the impact you want to make in the world. The purpose you awaken to may give you the title of mom, or healer, or artist, or non-profit founder, or political campaign leader. Whoever you discover you are, and whatever you're here on earth to do, you'll do it in your whole life, not just your work. This is important to know, because it gives you greater flexibility as we discover your next calling. Your next job doesn't have to be the exact right match for you. It can simply be the right next step. It still can be a vehicle for you to make the impact you want to make in the world.

Your future may hold surprises to you. By connecting with your purpose, without worrying about what your next job title is just yet, you'll open yourself up to unexpected outcomes. These outcomes may tickle and delight you in ways you never would have dreamed of.

Your Purpose Will Launch You into Action

At the same time your purpose will be opening you to some new possibilities, it will also close off others that aren't right for you. Knowing your purpose helps you narrow down what types of work you want, because it gives you a visceral knowing of how you want to feel, or how you want to be making others feel, or outcomes you want to be creating in the world. Without a visceral knowing of your purpose, you can spin indefinitely, entertaining various forward paths without any real sense of what is right for you.

When you connect with your purpose, you'll hear an internal "yes" as you look at some options, and an internal "no" when you look at others. You'll be seeing your options through the lens of your heart, the place of wisdom and intuition, which is often more dependable than logic alone. When you hear that *yes*, you can act on it and start creating your path forward. Acting on one *yes*, for example, might take you to a lecture on The Healing Potential of Massage Therapy. And at that lecture, you might get another *yes* at the opportunity to take the first course of a program led by the speaker. And at that program, you may get a *no* at the opportunity to become a licensed massage therapist, but as a result you may realize you're meant to help massage therapists get their businesses up and running. See how it works?

There are so many ways you can live your unique purpose. If you know what it is, you can start acting on it now.

Your Purpose Will Lift You Out of Burnout

Connecting to your purpose is so powerful that it can only lead you in a direction that fulfills you. If you've been suffering through work that makes you unhappy, and it's negatively impacted your wellbeing, your happiness, your self-image, or your relationships, you're probably longing for work that feeds and supports these things. And it's no wonder: You're headed for burnout, and that longing is your higher self, speaking up through instinct. You really do need to either get out fast, or drastically change your approach to your current work.

Most people think burnout comes from overwork, but that's not actually true. Burnout comes from overwork *without fulfillment*. You can work like a dog with a slave-driver mentality, forcing yourself through each day (which will cause burnout), or you can work like a dog because you're called and pulled forward by momentum and fulfillment. Sincere satisfaction and deep fulfillment are the antidotes to burnout. You don't need a job that's easier. An easy job that requires a lot of work will bore you. What you need is to be challenged. You need a job that calls you forth and feeds you at the same time.

Truly connecting with your purpose – not your company's purpose, and not the purpose you think you're supposed to have, but the actual purpose living inside you – will wake you up. It will ignite your curiosity (*What is possible?*) and your courage (*Can I really do this?*) and your willingness (*Who, me?*). Acting on your purpose will wash your burnout away like a heavy rain after a long draught.

Your Purpose Will Call You Forth

Your purpose has its wants for you, and it has its wants for others. At heart, your purpose is a function of generosity. It's the voice of your contribution. That voice may take you places you didn't think you would ever go. It may also take you well beyond what you ever thought you were capable of. When our hearts open up like this, and feel the extent and depth to which we really care, it moves us. We can't help but take action.

Whereas fear has held you back up until now, purpose will have you hitching your wagon to love and possibility. That wagon will carry you over and beyond your ego-concerns, and change your orientation to the world over time. For the sake of whom or what cause are you acting? Your purpose will hold a mirror up for you to see clearly, so you can relinquish habits based on fear-based thinking. It will lead you, over and over, into the growth needed for you to become the person your higher self knows you can be. Watching yourself rise to the occasion each time will give you a deep sense of satisfaction and trust in yourself.

Your Purpose Will Make You More Resilient

Something happens when you commit to following your purpose. Your purpose is more than a goal, or a destination, or an outcome. It is more about how you show up. It's the impact you want to make on your world, and it requires that you not only do certain things, but that you *be* certain ways. Because your purpose comes from such deep reservoir of care within you, you'll be accessing that care on a daily basis. The more you care, and the more committed you are to your purpose, the more grounded you will be.

I've always been a person with a lot of anxiety. I had panic attacks during my twenties, and until I realized I was a highly sensitive person, I had little way of making sense of why I was always trying to recover from my own emotions as well as witnessing emotions in those around me. The more I learned to stay connected to my core values, and see my emotional sensitivity as a leadership tool for me to master, the more grounded I became. I was able to do this because it was all for the sake of something I wanted to create, something I cared about – which was the power of love to heal, connect us, and create room for authenticity.

Your purpose will make you more resilient, because with every challenge you encounter – even the ones that have you quaking in your boots – you'll have a compelling reason to learn from it, rather than wallow in it or resist it. As you build that muscle of recovery over time, you'll recover faster and faster, becoming more and more resilient.

Trust Your Direct Experience for Purpose Is More than Intellectual

Engage Your Awareness and Listen to Feelings

Knowing your purpose takes awareness of what you care about. Pay attention to what you most emotionally respond to in the world around you. What pulls at your heart strings? You can care about certain causes deeply, but if you're always pushing those feelings aside, you won't connect the dots between your care and your purpose in life. When you do connect the dots, then you can start taking action. You can act on your purpose and begin to embody it in the work you do.

Allow for Vulnerability and Acknowledge Your Courage

As you uncover your purpose and embrace it, you'll be working from heart. Try to trust yourself enough to embrace change, however uncomfortable it is in this moment. If you can make friends with this vulnerability inside you, and learn to interpret it as a sign of courage and growth, you'll be able to lean into the changes you want more readily. Remember, resistance and vulnerability are natural, but they won't necessarily feel like it: They'll make you want to turn back, or hide, or talk yourself out of change. You've got to endure both to step into a life of fulfilling work.

How Alex Found Strength from His Purpose When Stakes Were High

Purpose can propel you much farther than you think you can go. My client, Alex, made major changes in his life just three months after beginning coaching with me and finding his purpose. When he connected with his purpose, he did so in such a deep way that it made no sense for him to stay in his situation – he knew he had to leave and start his own law practice to pursue his activist ambitions.

Alex recently came to a session with me with fears about an upcoming opportunity. He was asked to speak in front of Congress. Alex had by that time had plenty of practice being in the limelight. That wasn't the problem. The problem was that he couldn't figure out how to approach this talk he was asked to give, because he could only envision negative outcomes. He saw the drawbacks of any point of view he could present. He saw the potential for cynicism to knock down any appeal he tried to make. He saw his community railing against him if he made the wrong move and created an unintended negative outcome.

When we serve with purpose, we are called into situations that matter, situations where we feel there's a lot at stake. This was one of them for Alex. But Alex's perspective was getting in the way, lodging his focus on what was to be feared rather than what he wanted to create and how he wanted to show up. For Alex to figure these things out, he had to be a person who cared again, plain and simple. He had to forget about strategy and positioning – which arose out of the belief that he was boxed in. Instead, he had to step back and put that belief aside, and look at why he was doing this in the first place.

When Alex explored this, he saw that he was missing a huge opportunity by looking at things this way. When he connected back to his purpose – what mattered to him as a human being – he was able to form a more creative vision. He remembered that when Dr. Martin Luther King gave his "I Have a Dream" speech, he had just as much (if not more) reason to be cynical about a positive outcome given the climate then, but of course he gave the speech anyway. Alex saw that this was a chance for him to lead, by being honest and frank, and by letting his heart inform his beliefs of what was possible. This was an opportunity to call people forth into a bigger vision, one that existed for the greater good of all, and in order to feel grounded and clear (and be successful), he had to start there.

He did, by the way, and it worked. Alex felt he struck all the right notes, and was immediately invited to speak again, and the following month appeared as a special guest of the Council of the Americas on C-Span. His dedication to his ultimate purpose, to be a voice for people in Latin America, continues to pull him forward.

Take Action: Uncover Your Purpose by Exploring from Different Angles

Go to a comfortable place where you won't be distracted. I love to walk the woods when I'm noodling through a problem or connecting with my purpose. Use these questions to explore what's inside you. Your purpose is there – it's just waiting for you to embrace it.

What Drives You Crazy?

Even though it's a source of profound irritation, this response to an event or type of situation can help you get to the heart of what you care about. Start with what drives you crazy. What values of yours are being stepped over in that situation? Why is this issue so important to you? What does this say about what you care about, or how you're called to act?

What Vision of the Future Brings Feelings of Bliss?

You can find your purpose in your highest wishes for yourself and others. If you could change the world in any way, how would you change it? When you ask yourself this question, don't edit yourself. Allow any answer to be legitimate. Then take that, and explore it: What does this vision say about what you believe in? What does your bliss tell you about your core motivation in life?

What Breaks Your Heart?

We all have moments of breakdown – situations we can barely be with because they trouble us so. What have you witnessed in the world that truly breaks your heart? What can you barely tolerate? What gets you out of your chair and makes you want to start screaming into a megaphone? Sometimes our purpose comes from an instinct to protect others. Pay attention to your protective instincts. They will tell you a lot about what you're here on this earth to do.

Look to Your Wounds

Your own past can give you key insight into your purpose in life. We've all overcome struggles and healed wounds from the past. What have been the most important wounds that you've healed? Look at the motivation you had to heal those wounds. Look at what you learned in the process. How do all of those experiences – the wounding, the longing for healing, and the healing – set you up to make a difference? What are you uniquely prepared (and motivated) to do now because of them?

Pulling It All Together: Awaken to Your Purpose and Use It for Good

Before you set out to hunt for the perfect job, spend some time looking at who you are. When you get clear on the real source of your motivation and willingness to make an impact, you'll be better prepared to identify the right direction for you. You'll be out of the mindset of what you think you should do and into the mindset of what you feel called to do. You'll be much more courageous, powerful, and resilient as a change-maker that way.

Take time to let your paradigm shift from one of self-protection (based on fear) to one of empowered contribution. Make room for feelings of vulnerability, resistance, and disruption as you listen to your heart and acknowledge your purpose. Trust yourself, keep your eye on the future you want to create, and let your journey unfold.

Appreciate and Own
Your Magic

Everyone has their own brand of magic inside them – something that's unique to them – something they do without thinking about it, because it simply comes from who they are. A person can't hide their magic – it's always there, in plain sight. But that doesn't mean it's always easy for them to see. It's important that you see your magic, because it's part of how you'll know you're capable of making the impact you want to. It's also important because you'll be at your most fulfilled and most effective when you're in the zone of your magic. When you're looking for a new job, the more you can align your new role with your innate magic, the better.

Your magic may be hidden from your sight and if it is, that's making things harder than they need to be for you. We accumulate wounds throughout life that taint our perspective and sometimes cause us to look at reality (and ourselves) in skewed ways. This hides our magic from our view. It makes us tend to focus on what we lack, instead of how much we have to offer. I find that most of us don't really know what's so great about us. When we hear about it from others, it's incredibly moving. It's even hard to take in! We're not accustomed to seeing our own light with such clarity.

And yet when we *do* see our light, it can shift how we feel so much that we see the whole world differently. When you see yourself through a lens of lack, you'll look externally for ways to fill whatever hole inside yourself that's bothering you. You'll also have a tendency to see the world around you as lacking, because it's not filling that hole fast enough. There are problems every-where, and they keep us hard-working adults working very hard.

But when you see your light clearly, it's disarming. It makes all that work seem a little silly. You find out you're rich, when all this time you thought you were poor. Can you imagine how your life might change with a perspective shift like that?

That's why we're going to talk magic in this chapter. I would love for you to see yours. I'd love for you to see your riches, experience appreciation for them, and witness your impact on others. This is because I want you to know how powerful you are, so you can use that power for good.

Your Magic Is Hiding in Plain Sight

It's just not common for people to walk around seeing the absolute best in others and calling it out all the time. Most of us spend at least half our time thinking about what stresses us out. We're too occupied with our own needs to see anyone else. And that may be why your magic hasn't been mirrored back to you by the people around you. Trust me, they would if we got them all in a room and started talking about it together. Just because no one's telling you about the impact you make on them and how that impact makes them feel, doesn't mean you're not making it. It really takes stopping, being present, and being grounded in your own positive perspective to acknowledge the positive in others and not take it for granted. Life is complicated and we are distracted. For this reason, it can be hard to even know you're making a positive impact on someone, especially if you're not even trying!

It can also be hard to know you're making a positive impact if you're not reading the signs on other people's faces and in their actions. You can change the direction of someone's whole day with just one conversation. Because of you, they change their perspective on something important. They can feel better about who they are, and more accepted. They can feel comforted by your presence. They can feel reassured that they're doing the right thing. They can remember their strengths. Even if you don't actively try to create this change in others, you may be doing it without realizing it, *just by being you*. That smile on their face at the end of your conversation is there because of their emotions, but together you co-created those emotions in your conversation. That was your impact. If you're not paying attention, you can walk around thinking that what you do (or even who you are!) doesn't matter. Yes, that may be because no one is specifically thanking you. But it could also be that you're not noticing your effect on others. It could be that you're missing this opportunity without knowing it; you're not appreciating yourself.

When you don't see your impact and appreciate yourself, it's easy to create a story that you're invisible, or you don't matter, or you're unappreciated, or you're dispensable. And when you have that story in your mind guiding all your actions, it's hard to feel motivated to do anything at all. Studies show people are happiest at work when they're making progress. Work doesn't have to be enlightening, groundbreaking, or life-changing. The bottom line is that for us to be happy and feel like there's a reason for what we're doing, it really helps to see our impact. But so often we're missing it, because we're absorbed in our thoughts, or our stress, or our activities.

Even if you do know you matter and you do feel appreciated, you're reading this book because on some level, you're not living out your full potential. You're not seeing what you want of yourself. You're not feeling fulfilled by what you do. You're not making the impact you want to make. Seeing your magic helps you see your impact. They are one and the same. And when you know your magic, you can wield it more consciously to make the impact you want. There's no further degree required, no class, and no hiking up Mt. Everest needed. Your magic is already inside you, and taken care of. All you have to do is see it and own it.

Things Look Different When Seen Through the Light of Magic

Most clients who come to me wanting some kind of career change – so they can just do meaningful work and feel good about themselves – are approaching it from a problem-solving mindset. First, they want to pick the right job, then they want to get it. That may work for some, but if you're reading this book, odds are it's more complicated than that for you. Or maybe you don't see how it should be any more complicated than that, and so you've been beating yourself up for not being able to do it.

When clients first come to me, I usually spend time in the beginning getting really clear on their magic. What can I immediately tell about this person? I share it with them. I articulate it when I see it, sometimes in different ways or from different angles. I do this because most of us don't have that clear mirror of ourselves, and we don't necessarily have people around us who are experts at seeing and acknowledging us, either. What I see – even when I'm seeing something they see too – is often surprising to clients.

I have one client, Emelie, who came to me because, although she had a nice job and a nice boss, she was longing to be more outwardly authentic, showcase her creativity, and find freedom in more consultative work. In the first two sessions with Emelie, I was really struck by something about her that I couldn't quite name at first. I knew on a gut level that this client could get what she wanted – she could create anything she wanted – yet she was consumed with a lot of negative noise in her head that was getting in the way. So, despite her perceived barriers and her experience that getting what she wanted was difficult or next to impossible, I knew that was a false story. This is someone who had, in a year and a half, found her soul mate, started a family, and bought her first home. There was nothing stopping her. Emelie's magic is her power. She is a force to be reckoned with and when you're with her, you can feel this on a visceral level. No wonder she'd been promoted quickly in her field and awarded Employee of The Year by the organization she'd been working for.

Why is it important for Emelie to know her magic? Well, for one thing, if Emelie doesn't see her power, she's not as equipped to use it for good. There are two things that can happen if you don't see, acknowledge, and fully own your magic. One is: You'll likely project this quality onto other people, seeing this aspect of them, and pseudo-worshipping it. You'll use it to put those people above you, and just out of reach. Just like that, you'll separate them from you, and create a story about what you aren't. That leads to beliefs about what you think they're capable of, how lucky they are, and how you wish you were them in some way. When you *are* them. You are that magic. You have it too. You just haven't owned it.

So that leads you nowhere good. The story you create seems real to you, and it follows you around. No matter where you go, there's another one of those people, getting what they want and driving you crazy.

You can make yourself invisible that way. I know because I've done it, and it's not fun. That's the other thing that can happen if you don't fully own your magic. Not only will your magic be invisible to you, but it will be invisible to everyone else, too, most likely. You won't get the acknowledgment or opportunities you could have. In fact, your story about who you are will probably be reflected in how other people treat you. And that will make the suffering you feel about not being seen and not having opportunities seem intractable. It will seem like this story about how much you lack is written in stone and is absolutely true, when it's not. This feeling of powerlessness is extra suffering that I don't want you to have.

Knowing your magic and truly owning it can help you in so many ways. The biggest reason to get in touch with your potential for positive impact is that it helps you consciously engage this part of you. It is incredibly fun to build on your strengths, let yourself be you, and focus on what you possess to contribute. It's another way to keep your saboteurs at bay, so you can be the most effective version of yourself. It will take a lot of the feeling of struggle away, as you narrow in on work that would be truly meaningful for you and start creating it for yourself.

You Don't Need Armor When You Have Magic

I gave a workshop with a friend and colleague of mine (whose name is Michael) at a women's center once. The title of it was "Unleash Your Magic." We gathered in a circle with twelve women in their teens and twenties, all of whom had run from dangerous or violent situations, some of whom had small children, and some of whom had recently gone through rehab. After our introductions, I could tell the room wasn't ready to move forward. Each of the women had been volunteered, as we learned, and they weren't necessarily up for what we had to give. But they also didn't yet know what we had planned on giving.

It took some truth telling and frank talk about what we were about to do, and what it would take to make it work. If it worked, they were in for an incredible day. If they didn't commit – if they weren't up for what we were about them to do – the workshop wouldn't work. So it was their choice. They could decide to create with us, or they could opt out.

Everyone stayed, and we got to it. Our workshop involved using the entire group to see and draw out the unique "magic" of each woman there. Their "magic," as we framed it, was their natural impact. Everyone has a unique impact – like a fingerprint – on the people and the space around them, without even trying. Who you are naturally creates something. Some people naturally create uplift, because they're so drawn to humor. Some people create safety, because they're always telling the truth. Some people create beauty, because their presence is soft and reflective. Some people create inspiration, because they share what's in their heart even when it takes courage to do so.

With each woman, we found their magic and named it. It wasn't hard to do. We all used our intuition and our senses to see the person clearly. Even with those of us who had just met, we were able to do it. A person's impact is clear when you look for it, notice it, and start to speak to it. This process is incredibly empowering. But the irony is, it's also scary. It takes guts to see and own your own magic. It's one thing to tell someone else how fantastic they are and what they bring to the table just by being themselves. It's another thing to hear a room full of people describing your magic. For most people, it's harder to receive than criticism. In that moment, everyone experiences your impact together and sees the best in you. For twenty minutes, all you hear is how magical you are in this way … in these ways. All you witness is gratitude from others. There's no one to fight. No one to prove wrong. No one to prove yourself to. You are already seen, already noticed, already accepted, and already acknowledged.

It's Incredibly Disarming

When Michael and I gave this workshop to a group of leaders, we did a demo before the group got started, by having Michael lead the group in seeing and articulating my magic. About ten minutes into my turn, I had tears in my eyes. The room went quiet. All I saw were eyes filled with love while they noticed the emotion rising in me. I nodded my head, and met their eyes, just as we train participants to do – to fully receive what's happening. "Michael, I forgot how hard this is!" I said, and the whole group laughed. As facilitators, we come in wanting to give so much, and thinking it takes courage to lead a workshop like this, where our job is to hold space for all kinds of emotions. But the participants are the ones with the real courage, because they're the ones breaking free of their old story of not being good enough, being too much of this or too much of that, being held back, being dismissed ... whatever it is. It takes enormous courage to see and own your own light.

At the end of each person's turn, we have them step into the magic that they've just articulated is theirs. Ironically, not only is their magic a place of strength for them, but it's also a place of vulnerability. Everyone has a way of hiding their best gems, for fear of rejection, or criticism, or anything else. It is harder and takes more courage to own your greatest gift and allow it to be seen, than it is to work so hard to prove that you're good enough, or lovable enough, or just enough.

Accepting what is eminently lovable and filled with light inside you is how you begin to make your contribution. You must clear away the barriers you've inherited, or adopted, or made up to protect yourself, and get to what's shining already on the inside. You must do that so that you can offer it.

When I spoke with the director of this women's center over a year after our workshop, I got curious. I wanted to know if the workshop had lasting impact. She immediately piped back with praise, and an emphatic "We *still* talk about that workshop!" Once you light a flame inside you, then you know what it's like to have that flame lit. It's motivation to keep coming back to that place.

Your Magic Will Lighten Up Your Life

I've come to see that love is at the root of healing, it's at the root of change work, and it's at the root of good leadership. It's not a word we use in a professional context, and yet, if you don't love – if you're not using the skill of love in your work – you're probably not nearly making the impact you could be.

It takes love to connect with your magic, because you can only see your magic if you put on your own rose-colored glasses. You have to choose to see yourself through a lens of love in order to get anywhere with it. It's a big step, and I hope you keep taking it.

Because it takes love to see your magic in the first place, love is sparked, mobilized, and activated in the process. And anytime you call on your own inner resources of love – when you stop to look at the world through a loving lens – you will feel love. You'll be filled with the stuff. You'll also emanate it. You can't put on love-goggles to see your own magic and not start seeing magic all around you. It's a choice of perspective, and once you make it, everything changes. Choosing love changes everything.

If you do choose to look at yourself through the lens of love, and if you choose to look at others this way too, your experience of life will change. Your way of interacting with others will likely change. You won't want to get drawn into drama or negative self-talk, because it's just too good over here in magic land. Life is too short to waste on stuff that's not real anyway. Why not choose to see life, and yourself, and others, in a way that makes you tingle with delight?

Take Action: Open Yourself to Seeing Your Magic

Start paying attention to your impact on people. When you buy coffee at your local cafe, does the person waiting on you laugh or smile? When you have dinner with a friend, does her energy seem different at the end than it did at the beginning? When a coworker shares something in confidence with you, notice the impact you must have had until that point that laid the groundwork for her trust.

When are you at your best? Think of a moment when you knew something important was happening, or something felt magical. What was your contribution to that moment? What aspect of you, or your energy, do you think helped to create that?

Ask a handful of people what they think is truly unique about you – ask them: "What positive impact do you think I might make without knowing it?" Remember, it can be big or subtle. Sometimes a person can have a subtle magic that creates a big impact over time.

Putting It All Together: Appreciating and Owning Your Magic

You don't have to wait for your boss, or coworkers, or anyone else around you validate who you are and what your potential is. You can see your own light, and you can appreciate it. You can see your impact and own it. This way, you'll help yourself move forward, by knowing exactly what you bring and finding more places (like your dream job) to bring it. Owning your magic won't just make you more of a leader. It may even soften your perspective toward life, making it seem a whole lot more friendly.

Learn to see your magic, and remind yourself of it regularly. Make sure you put yourself in situations where your specific magic is needed. Practice using it with intention, and let yourself be seen. Build on it and expand it. Your magic is your superpower.

Welcome Your Emotions and Activate Your Inner Healer

If you're serious about making a big change in your life; if you know you want to blow through your own barriers and create what you don't yet believe is possible for yourself; then you're about to get to the core of change work. This chapter is about emotions and healing, and how they power change. You may wonder what emotions or healing wounds have to do with change work, or finding your dream job, or escaping your own self-made and self-limiting patterns. I'm going to show you in this chapter. This is for advanced and committed change-makers, and, if you've gotten this far in this book, you can count yourself among them.

Emotions aren't just something that are dealt with in a therapist's office, and healing doesn't only happen after reconciling differences. The power of emotions and healing is bigger than that. I believe the process of feeling and healing is at the heart of all change. Before something new is born, something must die. Before something new is embraced, something has to be let go. Before a new belief is set in place, the old one needs to be destroyed. These transformations require love, patience, and healing to be completed.

It's important for you to know that difficult emotions don't always indicate that something negative is happening. These emotions are often a sign that you're doing something right: You're growing and changing. If you shut them down without knowing it, or if you change course because you've interpreted them to mean something bad is happening, you may miss your chance at moving forward. If you're committed to becoming the person you know you can be, you're going to have to break through the patterns that have kept you in this same stale place, feeling held back from living your potential.

Do you find yourself fighting the same horrible boss, no matter what job you take? Do you find yourself coming back to the same circumstances over and over – like being betrayed, or being one-upped, or ignored? Is your creativity and willingness to rock your job always thwarted, no matter what company you work for? Is there a person in your life who's always triggering you and nearly driving you mad, but whom you can't let go of?

Getting stuck in a pattern is tough. It seems like everything you do, despite your very best intentions, brings you back to the same place eventually. You can start to wonder if you're cursed. Well, the secret to finally breaking those patterns that follow you is feeling and healing. Somewhere, that pattern emerged because you started unintentionally avoiding an experience or emotion. It's totally natural; when you started avoiding it, you did so unconsciously and for good reason. It's a protective mechanism.

But remember our protective mechanisms the saboteurs from Chapter 3? After they've served their purpose, they tend to keep us from growing. It's hard to know when you're stuck in a pattern of avoiding. But as a coach, I know how to spot it. I also know how to help you move beyond it, which I'll share with you.

In this chapter, I'll show you how you can break through these patterns. You're going to learn how emotions and healing operate in the context of change, how to spot opportunities for you to heal, and how to engage your own healing process for the sake of your growth. Some of this may be new to you. Some of it may sound weird. I encourage you to embrace it for the sake of creating the real change you want for yourself, even as you encounter difficult experiences. As you'll learn in this chapter, these are only experiences, and experiences always come and go. Resistance to experience, on the other hand, always makes it stay.

It's Time to Reframe How We Think of Emotions and Healing

Healing, like emotions in general, is commonly understood as being private, personal, and medical. From this perspective, healing is for when you're broken. But this is an unfortunate mischaracterization. Holding space for awareness, emotions, and love as we brave new challenges and heal old wounds is fundamental to welcoming change. Taking time to acknowledge what's happening for you and creating room for yourself to feel the emotions surfacing will feed the momentum of your change. It will make the transformation inside you real and permanent.

We've all had traumatic or dramatic experiences that have shaped who we are. As you take big steps toward your change that challenge your status quo, this may trigger fear, resistance, sadness, or any others of a host of emotions inside of you. What you're embarking on is a dramatic change. You'll need to acknowledge these responses and get comfortable around them, so you can use them to further your growth. Moments of hurt, while painful, often indicate opportunities for healing; they're a necessary stage in the passage of your journey. How you respond to these opportunities will determine how the story of your transformation will go.

The Change You Long for May Depend on Healing

Do you recall times when you have that thought: *I'll never be able to get what I want*? Well, in a way, that thought is right; you really *will* never get there, at least not from the place you are now. You have gone as far as you can with this set of beliefs, with this set of skills, with this *you* who you are now. To move beyond this place, a change needs to happen inside you. You'd be surprised how much of your external world will show up differently, just because you created a dramatic shift inside yourself. Don't ask me to explain it, I just know that it happens!

Healing parts of you that have been waiting to be listened and responded to creates seismic shifts in how you relate to the world. The best way I can say how healing creates a new you is this: Healing changes the past, which in turn alters your future. Sounds very *Matrix*, doesn't it? Let me explain.

Let's say you grow up with a parent who rages a lot. It's your mom, and she's got her own wounds, and she's doing the best she can, but she's losing it. You're a toddler, and you're on the floor in your diapers. You don't know what's happening, and you're scared. You're scared of the very person who helps you interpret the whole world. Biologically, your job is to eat, poop, sleep, and be loved. Those are all the things you need to survive, and you're fully equipped to do all of them. But for some reason, you're not getting loved. You haven't been alive long enough to do anything to make anyone as mad as your mom is right now. But you don't know that. Nothing makes sense, and in the ways that your biology can sense of the situation, your life is at stake.

In that moment, your protective mechanisms will swoop in and save you. Maybe they'll diminish your need for love and give you a blind spot, so that you don't perceive your own danger. Maybe they'll create a belief that you did something to make your mom mad, which gives you the perception that you can control the situation and get the love you need, by altering your behavior. Whatever it is, you have remarkable supports in your brain to keep you alive. Thank goodness for those.

But later, when you're older (and you're not a toddler anymore) and your safety isn't in danger, you're still operating with that same mechanism in place. It's just like what I described in Chapter 3 about Saboteurs. Only now, you have absolutely no experience with that emotion you saved yourself from having that was so dangerous as a toddler. You've protected yourself from feeling unloved, and made it a really scary thing to feel. Probably scarier than it would be if you just felt it.

Without realizing it (because you've always had these mechanisms, and never really known differently), you go through life avoiding situations in which you might feel unloved. Maybe you avoid falling in love. Maybe you avoid expressing love. Maybe you avoid jobs where your heart is really in it, which gives you a safe emotional distance from everything work-related. Everything you do and every choice you make falls under these conditions: They're ok as long as they don't create an experience where you will feel unloved.

Then, as a result of this, you can't seem to figure out why you can't find a lasting partner. Or, you can't figure out how other people can be such rock stars at work, doing what they love and being recognized by everyone around them. Or, you can't figure out why you feel like you're unlovable. None of these things will seem like they're results of your choices or your beliefs. They'll happen as if magically. Your partner will lose interest before the relationship moves to the next level. The company you work for will go under, leaving you to start your job search again before you get to establish yourself. You'll keep encountering people who are downright mean. None of this is within your control, right? And yet, the pattern is recognizable.

You can do everything in the world to try to change things, but this same darn situation will keep coming back. That's because you're living out your future from the point of view of the past, as it stands with you now. You're living out: *I am unloved.* Every act of yours is infused with the perspective of *I just want to be loved.* Your life is about going out and getting that love, because from where you are, that's the missing piece. That's the hole to be filled. That's the thing that will make you complete.

Here's what life will give you in response to that: the same experience over and over again, until you go back and fix the past. When you go back and fix the past, when you take the core wound – that core wounded girl inside you – and respond to her with humanity, empathy, and grace, you will change your operating system. You'll change her experience. And by changing her experience, you open up a whole new future. You completely change her story. When you finish what was started – when you flood her need for love with love, the book closes. *Thank you,* your younger self says. *What a relief,* your future self says. The pattern stops. New life emerges.

Healing plays a role in what and how much we are able to be and do in this world. If you want to create big change in the world, if you are daring enough to try, you must add healing to your change-making tool belt. You must know how to heal yourself, and you must be able to recognize and respond to the need for healing around you.

How to Activate the Healer Within You

Look to the Wisdom of Your Heart-Based Emotions

If you've had a past trauma or dramatic event, it's likely that you learned to protect yourself from experiences by going into your head. Over time, if you've had a few of these events in the past, you'll start to live in your head. You'll over-rely on your intellect for guidance, especially when you feel vulnerable. Your heart doesn't see vulnerability as a problem or threat like your head does. But for that reason, it's important to shift into your heart for direction and guidance. This takes courage at first. Moving into your heart when you're most motivated to stay in your head (because you feel vulnerable) takes a lot of consciousness.

But as we've seen with Robyn, moving into your heart is just the thing you want to do. It makes the insights and wisdom you have within you accessible. Did you know that your heart is a brain? According to research done by HeartMath Institute, the heart has 40,000 neurons within it that communicate to your brain. When you activate heart-based emotions like compassion, care, joy, or appreciation, those neurons fire up, and as a result, your brain behaves differently, helping you access more of your inner resources. Understanding that your heart is a resource that is always there for you to draw upon will help you use your heart to navigate stress on a daily basis.

Mobilize Your Observer to Ground and Guide Yourself

In order to use your heart most effectively, you'll need to engage your observer. Your observer is simply the part of you who can say things like, *I'm observing myself feel sad. I'm observing tightness in my chest. I'm observing my mind go blank. I'm observing that my left foot is itchy.* You'll need your observer because – and this is important – emotions will pass through you when you feel them but avoid getting caught up in the story you think they tell. You'll need to brave new emotional experiences without interpreting them as bad, or threatening, and without judging yourself as bad, weak, or threatening for having them.

I've had clients, for example, who avoided feeling rage as a result of their experiences at work (when they get triggered by a coworker, for example). It's definitely helpful to regulate your emotions and express them appropriately, but it's also helpful to allow those feelings to come and go at least privately. Rage is just an emotion, and it's one that will pass through us soon enough, if we allow ourselves to feel it. When my clients eventually allow themselves to feel more range of emotions, they come away with a clearer understanding of themselves. They might acknowledge their values and where they need to take more of a stand, for example. As a result, they feel a sense of freedom and release, because they've stopped using their energy to resist themselves. If you always attach meaning (particularly negative meaning) to your feelings, it can cause you to resist them. It's a lot easier to see emotions as energy, color, or temperature even, moving through you like a hot flash, than it is to deal with the sensations of those emotions and also manage your interpretation and resistance to those experiences. Keep it simple. Postpone meaning-making until you're on the other side, experiencing some peace.

If you're not used to engaging your observer, I recommend trying any meditation course (or the Headspace app) to get used to the process. The more you practice this, the easier it gets. Using your observer over time will help you integrate and improve communication between the different quadrants of your brain, making you less reactive and more nimble. It's probably one of the most basic yet powerful practices you can use to become a more resilient leader. (See *Mindsight*, by Daniel Siegel.)

How June Discovered Her Inner Resources and Surprised Herself

My client June wanted to explore what she wanted for her future, yet she struggled with the unknown. This was something that held her back: When she looked forward in life, she couldn't see anything. She had trouble accessing her own vision of her future career, yet she saw friends around her knowing what they would do and already enjoying success. Her instinct was to panic and "figure it out" by seeking solutions, just like any other problem – thinking it through, looking for answers and strategies, and trying to fix what she felt was wrong. For her, signs of the unknown meant that she was in the wrong place. It meant she wasn't enough, wasn't finished, and was on the wrong track. Being in the unknown was the experience June had been working hard at avoiding without realizing it.

As a consequence, June would find herself doing busywork. Distracting herself from what was really important – pondering her future – she'd focus on things like social media and easy tasks that gave her a temporary feeling of victory. But all that busywork used up her energy, and made her feel even more detached from her real value and potential to create change in the world. As time went on without making the real progress she wanted, she felt lost, and on top of that, critical of herself for being so.

Session after session, here's what I witnessed: A few moments of heart-based breathing took June out of the spin-cycle of her thoughts, and grounded her in her body and wisdom. In about a minute she could go from feeling lost to finding perspective again.

When I took June through a visualization into an imaginary space where she would truly experience the unknown, the very thing she was afraid of, something new spontaneously emerged for her. That space of the unknown went from being terrifying and alienating, to being still, soft, and warm. She experienced her own healing mechanisms coming forward to comfort her. Beneath her fear was wisdom and peace, two things she'd never associated with being in the unknown before. She witnessed her own capacity to heal, and it amazed her. She felt tingly, and loved, and warm, and safe.

This is how healing happens! Our bodies have a natural tendency to heal. If we stay present, and allow ourselves to experience the moment, wisdom will show up. As coach, I know I don't have to do anything to make that happen; my job is to hold the space and help my client stay present. I never know what wisdom will emerge from within the client. I just know that something will. It always does.

Healing Will Help You Unlock Doors of Opportunity

While you can spend a lifetime resisting a certain experience, and suffering as a result, it doesn't always take that long to heal. Sometimes healing can happen in a matter of moments. Sometimes it happens spontaneously. What can you expect as a result?

You can expect your life to change! You can expect that barriers you thought you'd never move through move aside. You can expect to make the changes you don't yet think are possible for yourself. You can expect to experience your own wholeness and freedom again. You can expect that you will start knowing on a visceral level that you can handle whatever comes your way.

This is where you'll start to see real movement forward. Unleashed from the tethers that kept you down in the past, you'll see yourself heading into new situations and challenges you wouldn't have dared entered before. You'll both surprise yourself, yet also have the feeling that you always knew you could do it.

Not only that, but your relationship to your past will change. Your memory of the past may in fact change. You just won't be the same person after you heal. After I healed so many wounds in the span of a couple years of massive breakthroughs, I found that I couldn't really remember what it used to be like to be me. I could remember words that I'd used to describe what I felt at the time, but I couldn't really remember the feeling.

Physiologically, I changed, and you may experience this too. It's as though I'd had a complete cellular makeover. Before these transformative experiences, I'd suffered from migraines every month, landing me on the couch for a few days each time, and now I don't get them anymore unless I travel by plane. Even then, I don't always get them. I haven't refilled my migraine medicine prescription in over two years!

Take Action: Evoke Your Inner Healer

Open a journal and explore areas where you get hung up. Look for clues to how healing might be a part of your journey. Imagine what would be possible if you healed the wounds that are governing your responses to the world.

What circumstances do you find yourself in again and again, no matter how hard you try to avoid them?

What emotional or sensory experiences are those circumstances helping you avoid?

What experiences trigger you? What emotions do they evoke?

How are you with those feelings? Do you run from having them? Where do you abandon yourself?

Who would you be without those patterns or trigger responses? How would your experience of life change?

Based on your answers above, what part of you is crying out to be healed? What does that part of you want or need?

Allow this part of you to experience that longing while you observe with compassion. Invite her to speak to you and ask for what she needs. Then, with your adult self, soothe this part of you and give her what she's been asking for. Do it in any way you can think of: this may mean speaking to this part of you inside your imagination as you hug a pillow, or it may mean taking a day off to rest, or it may mean making an effort to be extra patient and gentle with yourself. There's enormous wisdom in these wounded parts of yourself. Let them speak to you, so you can respond with healing intention and action.

The next time you get triggered, and have a dramatically negative response to something, use it as an opportunity to heal. Activate your observer, and hold yourself with love. Know you're strong enough to have this experience, and do your best not to resist it or run from it, but stay in it. All experiences pass eventually. Only resistance makes them stay.

Pulling It All Together: Welcome Your Emotions and Activate Your Inner Healer

Healing isn't for the sick and injured, it's for all of us. Emotional experiences are part of life, and we need to work with them skillfully in order to be capable change-makers. How you relate to the wounds of your past will shape how you relate to your future. If you don't want your future to be as limited as your past, I encourage you to embrace your own healing. Embrace your heart as a tool, engage your observer as your ally, and give your soul the closure it needs to move forward. Love what needs to be loved in you. Hear what needs to be heard. See what needs to be seen. When you're able to come through like this for yourself, you'll have the courage to come through for others, too.

Step Three in Creating Change: Choose to Act on Your Beliefs

You've expanded your belief in possibility through awareness, vision, and commitment. You've tapped into belief in yourself through your purpose, magic and healing process. You've shed layers of limiting thoughts and behaviors and replaced them with ones that bring you to life. Congratulations! You've made it to Step 3 – Choose to Act on Your Beliefs.

In the last part of this book, you'll learn to make it all real. Choosing to act on your beliefs means you'll be saying out loud, "This is what's about to happen for me." You won't wait for permission from anyone else, and you won't wait to be invited. You'll be the first to say you believe it's possible to find out what kind of work would make you feel at ease in your strengths, and like you're making a difference, and you'll take action.

In Part 3, I'm going to show you how acting on your belief in possibility creates magic. You don't need to know how you'll do something to know that you'll do it. You just need to act on your belief that *This is so*, and you will figure it out. Answers will appear. Paths will present themselves. Your belief, combined with your commitment to acting on it, will take you into new territory, and that's how you'll create this change that's eluded you for so long until now.

In Chapter 9, I'll walk you through how to engage action as a creative force already alive in you (not just a to-do list). In Chapter 10, we'll review internal barriers, how they can pop up out of nowhere to derail you, and how to use them to further your growth. And in Chapter 11, you'll take a look at your new story: the new you that you'll be stepping into, equipped with a whole new landscape, and a whole new set of possibilities. Each of these chapters will help you make the choice, over and over, to act on your beliefs in what's possible.

Act on Your Inspirations to Build Momentum

So far, you've been learning how to support yourself with empowered thinking, clarifying your vision of the future, and acknowledging your power to make a difference. As a result, there's a change happening inside your consciousness. This is an important change. It's this change – the one inside you – that will make your external changes productive and permanent. It's also this change that will allow you to keep growing, evolving, and marching forward into the meaningful work that you long for.

To empower that change, you'll want to pair it with action. The most important thing you can do is stay centered in a place of positive expectation of your future, and keep a grounded and positive perspective about your abilities so you can act on them. Every action you take from this place will both reinforce what's possible and move you closer to your dream. Action that you take from a saboteur perspective, on the other hand, will most likely move you away from it. Usually, my clients feel they need to plan out all the steps to reach their goal, and that without this plan they have no way of getting there. But the truth is, you don't need things planned out that far in advance. You only need to make sure you're acting from an empowered place, and that you're taking risks and trusting yourself.

What happens when you start believing in your dream and you awaken to your strengths, purpose, and values, is that you'll naturally feel inspired to do something about it. You'll think of something you want to try, or a step you want to take. Every time you act on these kinds of instincts, you'll be solidifying change. You'll awaken more and more parts of yourself, and one action will lead to another. Each week, you will be a little different. Each month, your life will change in some way as a result. Over time, you'll find yourself in a completely different place, looking back in wonder at how you made it all this way. When you choose to act on your beliefs in possibility, change just happens!

With all this inspired action (whether those actions are big or small), you'll be creating two things: 1) *your own becoming* (you're becoming the person you always knew you could be), and 2) *your ideal outcome*: a life of meaningful work. I don't think you need to worry too much about what actions you'll take. I find that when our barriers have been dismantled, ideas flood in and inspiration moves us. As long as you are summoning courage, taking new risks, and acting on what you believe is possible, you will be creating change.

That said, I do want to share with you a way of looking at action that may help you long-term. Since we tend to over-focus on pushing ourselves into action, I'm going to offer you a way of thinking of action that is a different approach. This other approach focuses on supporting you as a whole person, so that you sustain your energy and well-being along the way, while always keeping your door open to learning and developing.

Action Helps You Take Charge of Your Dream

There are two ways you can approach action, directly and indirectly. Direct action is the way we usually approach doing things. We mark down the steps moving us in a straight line, and go for it one by one. You'll use this whenever you want to get something done where there's little need for change, magic, or miracles. Direct action is great when the outcome is clear, and the process is linear. I don't find I need to teach anyone this – it's what we know already.

Indirect action is what you do when you need a small miracle. Indirect action helps you create the context for what you want to happen. Let's say you're inviting people over to fundraise for a cause or project you care about, and you know you want their help. There's setting the date, sending the invitation, and making your pitch. Those are direct actions. But then there's everything you can do to craft the outcome you want. Your task is really to move the hearts and minds of human beings, and so simply checking off a list of tasks alone may not get you there. So then you can explore: *What needs to happen for hearts and minds to be moved? What do my guests need to feel? What do they need to know? How do I need to show up? What do I need to do before-hand to show up that way?* This kind of exploration will give you a list of things to do to create a feeling of connection and generosity, if that's where you want to take people. It will also tell you what you need to do to *be the person* you need to be for this miracle to happen.

You can also use action to keep whatever change you want to happen for yourself moving along. If you're practicing moving into your heart in your work – because after years of working in a stressful environment you have a habit of closing if off – you can take action that would activate your heart more often. This could be anything from volunteering in your neighborhood, to getting a dog, or carrying a photo of your kids in your pocket every day. By doing these things, you'll build positive momentum toward becoming the you that you know you can be. You'll also be creating change in your neural pathways and building new habits. This change will make certain direct actions – that may have been intimidating to you before – start to feel accessible, or even easy.

Care for Your Dream by Approaching Action Holistically

As you dream about your future life, connect with your purpose, become aware of your magic, and set out to disrupt patterns, all the inspiration you feel along the way is fodder for action.

As you start to feel energized, or positive about the future, take any action that will keep you engaged with these parts of yourself. Choose actions that help you expand and move forward. Change is a creative process, and if you've been stuck, any action that you take from a place of positive emotion, hope, trust, or joy, will help you start to build momentum.

Use action as a tool to explore, play, and experiment. Use it intentionally as a way to give yourself experiences you want or need to have. Take action every week. Take action every day. Remind yourself that you are at choice and can use your creativity to create what you want!

Let's explore a list of examples of actions you might use to help yourself get unstuck and into inspiration and action, so you can realize your dream of finding meaningful work.

Practice Self-Reflection

As you do the exercises in the book, and connect with the insight and knowing that's already inside of you, you'll be able to clarify what to do next. Journaling, reflecting in nature, and generally taking time out and slowing down may, ironically, speed your growth. Self-reflection is like mental and emotional hygiene. It keeps you clear and connected to yourself, so you're ready to move forward.

Feed Your Soul

Many people who've been in the wrong job for years have been starving themselves in terms of fulfillment, self-care, and inspiration. It's hard to move forward when you're not fully activated (or you're nearly half-asleep). On the other hand, when you do things to feed your soul, you wake up and gather new energy. That energy is a valuable resource you can put to use in how you make a difference.

Expand Your Comfort Zone

Another contributor to staying stuck is staying comfortable. In that case, even if you're not sure of your next career move, in the meantime, you can challenge yourself in other ways. Do things that activate you and move you beyond your fears. Choose actions that are meaningful or fun for you, whether that's white-water rafting, volunteering abroad, or joining a public speaking group.

Deepen Your Relationships

As you connect with your purpose and allow yourself to dream big, you'll be discovering parts of yourself that had been latent, or just waiting to be seen. Share those parts with others. Open your heart, and connect over the things you care about. Deepening relationships in this way helps us form the kind of community that is essential to supporting courageous change. You'll need help along the way, and others will need your help, too. Actions that help you form new relationships and deepen old ones in this way will also keep you committed to living your purpose.

Follow Your Creative Impulses

Even if you don't know your next big move – and *especially* if you don't know your next big move – you can listen to your instincts and follow them. For example, if you're used to approaching your life decisions from your head (where your saboteurs live) and you're opening up to listening to your heart, your heart may have some surprising things to say. That's because our hearts are intuitive, and intuition doesn't always make clear sense to us when we first listen to it. Only acting on it will give you more clarity. Consider it a fun and curious exercise to say *yes* to your urges, no matter where they take you. No matter what happens, you'll learn about yourself in the process.

Never Stop Learning

You likely have learning and development activities associated with your job already. But consider what would happen if you allowed yourself to get a little outside the box with this. As you create the future you want for yourself, how might you want to expand the tools in your tool belt? What could you learn that would help you move forward on your journey or clarify your focus? What have you been dying to learn, but haven't yet? How might that relate to your next steps? Sometimes divergent thinking – or, in this case, acting – can help us piece together the vision we're longing for, by filling in the missing pieces needed to see a path forward.

Grow Your Spiritual Self

Since you're serious about living and working from your purpose, you're likely bringing deeply held beliefs about humanity into your new life. What are those beliefs? Finding your purpose and living it often involves spiritual development, not just personal development. If you find yourself attracted to activities that help you grow spiritually, I definitely recommend embracing them. Some of the greatest leaders of our time have been able to follow their dream of a better world because of their spiritual beliefs and practices. Give yourself permission to embrace and follow your longing for spiritual growth. It will be an important addition to the supports you lean on in your journey

Inspired Action Will Help You Create a New Reality Over Time

Taking action before you have everything figured out, as a way of engaging in the process of becoming, will change your experience almost immediately. If you've been truly stuck, you may have been harboring beliefs that it's impossible to get what you want, or even to experience what you want in life. You're like a sleeping giant, with incredible power to make a difference but stuck in stasis. Taking action on your belief in possibility will start to awaken you.

You'll Feel Sweet Relief

As you choose to act on your belief in possibility and your belief in yourself – even if it's more trust that you're acting on than it is belief – you'll experience how the reality you dreamed of is real, and true, and possible. This is what happens when we create change that we've dreamed of, but never created before. You'll feel enormous relief knowing that your saboteurs really were just voices of fear, and not true reflections of reality.

You'll Have Renewed Energy

As you start to create real change in your experience and gain felt clarity about your purpose, you'll find yourself renewed with energy. The heaviness you felt wasn't permanent, and it wasn't a sign of age. It was a sign of the presence of saboteurs. Saboteurs make everything hard, slow, and heavy. When you're operating from your heart, and your powerful self, things tend to feel imbued with vulnerability and joy. That's the stuff that will keep you on the edge of your seat. Because it takes courage, following your heart will feel exhilarating at times.

You'll Adopt Positive Expectations

Because you'll be acting from your heart, where all the positive heart-based emotions like appreciation, gratitude, compassion, and joy live, you'll experience an uplift in your attitude.

Acting on your heart's desire will, in turn, keep you connected to your heart, which will inform even more of your future actions. It's like a giant spiral moving upward. You'll be more successful at creating positive experiences for yourself and, as a result, you'll find yourself having more positive expectation (instead of negative forecasting) about the future.

You'll Experience New Confidence

The more creative you get with action, the more confidence you will build. Confidence comes when you know you don't need to avoid failure or unintended negative outcomes in order to survive. That's because you know you have the ability to recover from setbacks and correct mistakes. You've developed such comfort using action as a tool to create what you want that you claim a calm confidence in your abilities.

Take Action: Allow Yourself to Be Inspired into Action

Brainstorm a List of Actions that Resonate with You

What actions have you been inspired to consider while reading this book? Which ones excite you the most? Which ones scare you a little? Make a list now, and take ten minutes to brainstorm other actions you might take. Remember, you're using action as a creative tool, not a way of rushing yourself, or doing what you "should" do. Don't edit yourself. Write everything that comes to mind, no matter how nonsensical it may sound.

Commit to the Actions That Most Inspire You

Next, circle three actions that activate the biggest response in you. Use these three in the commitment stage of this exercise: What would it take to initiate each of those actions or projects today? What is the very first step? Next, get started. Take the first step to each action or commitment this week. If it can be done now, do it now. If it will take more time, plan a time on your calendar when you'll do it, and tell a friend who can hold you accountable at the end of the week.

The sooner you act on your intuition and inner knowing, the sooner you will experience the benefits!

Pulling It All Together: Act on Your Inspirations to Build Momentum

There are two ways of using action as a tool for moving forward. Direct action is the direct route to an end result that's concrete, measurable, and repeatable. Indirect action is what you use to navigate the unknown, when answers aren't clear and outcomes are a crap-shoot. Indirect actions support you as the main actor. They help you to grow and create the conditions for your success.

Act on your inspired belief in yourself and what is possible as much as you can, whether those actions are small and supportive or big and transformative. Taking action is a way of taking full responsibility for your experience of your happiness and your success. Consider taking action that helps you meet your needs for self-care, wellbeing, confidence-building, skill development, or inspiration to be productive to your role as change-maker. Consider taking action that challenges you to grow, or venture into new territory for the sake of learning and changing. Listen to where your intuition and wisdom is pointing you and meet that inspiration with action.

Trust Yourself to Move Through Internal Barriers

Once you commit to living a life of purpose, you'll begin to make changes – inside and out – that disrupt your status quo. As soon as you do that, chaos will greet you. You'll feel turned upside-down, it will be hard to make sense of the emotions happening inside you, and you'll be tempted to doubt yourself. Take heart! These are signs of change. Your brain is reorganizing how it understands you and the world. It's going to feel bumpy while you do all this changing.

This will be prime time for your saboteurs to come in and try to take over. They'll be very uncomfortable with what you're doing, and unable to see a path to possibility and success. And since you'll feel vulnerable, you'll be tempted to trust them. Try to keep your observer active, and resist the instinct to rip yourself out of the discomfort of the unknown!

Just when you're in the most chaos, the most discomfort, and feel the most like you don't know what you're doing, that's when change is happening inside you. You're forming new ways of being and new possibilities of the future for yourself. If you can do your best to stay in your experience instead of trying to find your way out of it or a way to fix it, you will keep the door to change open. You'll stay present to yourself and be able to answer the needs of different parts of who you are, which are now speaking up.

If you experience dramatic events, or intense resistance, or you get triggered, these are all things that are on your path so that you can grow. Every experience you have can be used as a way to become clearer, more loving and accepting of yourself, and more fit to reach your goal. If you allow moments like these to teach you, you will keep moving up and up and up and up, closer and closer to the future you desire. You'll free yourself in the ways you've been longing for.

The trick is to not see it as something that's wrong, or stopping you, or a sign that this whole thing isn't going to work. You'll be tested. It's part of every hero's journey. What you do with the test matters…a lot! That's what we're going to talk about in this chapter: how to work with internal barriers so they bring you closer to the future you want.

Internal Barriers May Suck, But They Don't Have to Stop You

When something comes up for us emotionally that knocks us off center, we want to fix it right away so we can get back to normal. But when it comes to these experiences, they're happening for a reason, and they are an opportunity for growth. It doesn't matter what sphere of life they're happening in. When you change, grow, and expand in one area, you'll likely apply that growth and expansion to many, many other areas, too. It's always worth it to choose to grow through what is happening. You won't just get better at handling this problem. In the end, you will be better at handling a host of problems.

That said, I'm a personal growth junkie and even I don't deal with all my barriers alone. I'm a coach, and I make full use of coaches myself because I want to always be moving myself forward. The ability to always be moving forward is my wish for you, too. There's no reason for internal barriers to stop you. Go get the right kind of help for you, whether that's a mentor, advisor, therapist, or coach. In my coaching practice, I love helping clients make use of experiences that derail them like: procrastination, fear, getting triggered, having a life crisis, inability to make decisions, self-doubt, getting blindsided, etc. The impact is like a double whammy: They get to both move through the trouble spot, and they get to make some permanent change in the process. Find the person or group that is right for you, to hold space for your learning and development.

Internal Barriers Will Come Bearing Gifts

Sometimes when we set an intention for ourselves, it's still conceptual to us because we still have a lot of growing to do to before we get there. By some miracle of how the universe works, the experiences we then have or face in life will be just the thing we need to grow in the way we need to grow. I'll give you a super dramatic example (but remember barriers present in more everyday shapes and sizes too). When I was in my 30s, I really wanted to figure out what my (life's) work was. I wanted to know where I belonged professionally, I wanted to know my value (my real value as a person, not what I was paid), and I wanted to make a difference. I was lost at the time. I had pieces of these things in my life at the time, but I was not happy, and not really moving forward.

Then an old boyfriend arrived on the scene, and soon I was engaged to be married. We'd set the date, booked the venue, sent out the engagement party invites, bought the dress ... but I was not destined to marry this man. He arrived in my life for a very good reason, and I was eternally grateful in the end that he did, but as it turned out, it was just not a good idea for me to move forward. That event forced me to get to know who I really was in the span of about six months. And boy did I get to the core of it. In full-on crisis mode, filled with fear, and anxiety, and confusion, I reached out to all kinds of supports, experts, and books, to make sense of what was happening to me. As I sorted it out, I did guided meditations. I focused completely on taking care of myself and listening for guidance.

And guidance came. In a park in Philadelphia, at about 10am while sitting on a bench, I heard clearly: *You are okay. You were always okay. You will always be okay.* Looking back, I can see that the real message (which I felt viscerally) was *You are loved. You were always loved. You will always be loved.* Big stuff to realize over coffee on a public park bench! Over that period of months, I realized that this was what I was about. More than anything else, love is what mattered to me. Not just the romantic kind. I'm talking about the kind of love that connects all human beings to one another. The kind of abiding, unconditional love afforded to us all, because it's what makes us human.

I felt this viscerally, physically, and knowingly, in a way I never had before. And yet it also felt as though I was remembering the truth, not stumbling upon for first time. My whole world changed as a result of this. I knew my value, as a person. I knew my purpose. I knew how to fill myself up and give myself what I needed emotionally – I simply had to turn to the love inside me. I knew that whatever I did in life, I wanted it to be about love.

And that's when I discovered coaching. I read about it in a leadership book and the language resonated with me like I'd always been speaking it. I knew in my heart and in my belly that this was what I wanted to do. This is what I was meant to do.

It took a year or so before I enrolled in my first coaching training program, but there it was. Everything that was unclear to me was made clear in about six months, and all as a result of a life crisis. The biggest kind of "barrier" there is.

I don't recommend praying for a life crisis, and you definitely don't need one to have the revelations you want. But life will give it to you if you're not moving along using your own methods. You'll get exactly what you asked for, but in a surprise package. And of course, crises also happen just because they happen. And we can use those, too, to become more of who we want to be. Humility is an important component of growth and confidence. It keeps us open, which is how we need to be when embracing any change.

How to Turn Internal Barriers into Personal Upgrades

Be with Your Experience

Just like we talked about in the chapter on emotions and healing, the most important thing to do is to remember to stay in your experience, whatever it is. When I've been majorly disrupted by something or someone who triggered me, it's taken me three days to a week to remember that I'm not supposed to escape this experience – I'm supposed to experience it. The way I know is that the more I try to flee, the more stuck I feel. I go in circles with it.

If you can catch yourself, and remind yourself to observe your experience, and stay in it, the experience will shift. Emotions and sensations don't stick around when you embrace feeling them. Only resistance will make them stay. The first step to working with any kind of barrier that shows up for you is to observe what's happening, label it, and try to let yourself experience it.

Don't Make Up Stories

The next step, once you've allowed yourself to stay put and experience what's happening in the moment, is to choose not to *interpret* what's happening. Wanting answers, wanting to understand, and wanting to make clear sense of what's happening is so normal, but it can be a way of denying yourself the experience. It is your hope of feeling instant relief that will make you want to understand everything and tie it up with a bow, but remember that you're strong enough to experience discomfort.

Like everyone who has ever lived, I get triggered by things people say sometimes. The self-righteous story I want to badly to make up in times like this is that this person is, of course, bad and wrong. But I also know, in my heart of hearts, that this isn't the case. The person involved is usually someone I love and respect. And my biggest and deepest value is love. So in order to stay true to myself, I have to love this person. I have to not "bite the hook," as Pema Chodron says. I have to find a way through this experience that both allows me to heal what needs to be healed and learn from it. When at my most hurt, it's taken me months to grow through it, yet I've learned things I never would have learned had I fallen for my first interpretation of the event.

The opportunity you have when a barrier shows up is to approach it differently than you have before. And that means, when you're stressed out or even in fight-or-flight, you need to create an opening. Just find a way to leave the door open for awareness. You don't have to make meaning happen, and you don't have to rush it. If you stay in the experience, your experience – and your way of seeing things – will shift.

Trust in Positive Outcomes

Trust that, when you get rocked, or blocked, there is an answer to your question around the corner. Use all the skills you've learned in this book to make sure you're centered in your heart, and being who you want to be in this process. You can't undo whatever just happened to rock you, but you can definitely grow and change your experience of it.

Imagine that this experience is the perfect opportunity for you, and it's been given to you, to help you get what you want or to grow in ways you've been longing for. Get curious and ask: what are some ways in which this might be true? How might this experience be happening for you and not to you?

Celebrate Your Ability to Outgrow Old Limits

By now you get that your internal barriers aren't showing up to make you miserable, they're here to help you move forward. And when you approach them in that way, so many good things will happen. For one, once you've made it through to the other side, you'll feel liberated. Not only will you have resolved your situation, but you will have changed. You outgrew your old limits, and as a result of that, so much more is available to you. This is freedom! You're free to be who you want to be – your best self.

Every time you allow yourself to have feelings you didn't before, or you forgive yourself and love yourself in a way you hadn't before, or you own some part of yourself you'd been afraid to look at before… you heal a fracture. You put yourself together again, and as a result you'll feel less divided, less like you're missing something, and more in touch with your innate value. This is how we reestablish our feelings of wholeness. It's a wonderful feeling.

Once you know how to navigate sticky places like these by staying true to yourself by courageously staying in your experience, and overcoming your internal barriers, you'll do it quicker and with more ease each time. This is like resilience training. You will need less and less time to recover from triggers and setbacks.

Pulling It All Together: Trust Yourself to Move through Internal Barriers

You can use all your life as a chance for you to become more of who you are. Not just the good times. Not just your wins. But all of it. Using all of life as your teacher will make you a brilliant and heart-centered change-maker. You'll keep yourself on track, and begin to truly know that, whatever comes your way, you will be fine. You'll recover and create what you want from it.

When something turns you upside-down, get the guidance you need to use it as a learning opportunity. You'll emerge different, new, and closer to your ultimate goals for yourself. There is a reason for everything, and that reason becomes more obvious the moment we start looking for it.

Get Ready for the New Version of You

Every new beginning starts from some other
beginning's end.

– Seneca

By now, you've made it through looking at your thinking and self-talk, you've dared to dream for what you really want (not a watered down version of it), you've been courageous enough to open your heart and see your purpose in the world, you've owned your magic when everything in you probably told you it was silly, you've responsibly taken on the support of using heart-based emotions to calm and heal yourself when needed, and you've committed yourself to moving forward and beyond internal barriers as they show up.

You've started a journey. You've initiated a change just by reading this book. With this chapter, we're going to acknowledge what this really means. What is really happening as a result of reading this book and internalizing new perspectives? What are you now starting to let go of? What new possibilities are you now aware of? Which of your strengths are you ready to more fully step into? What actions are you ready to take?

In this final chapter, we'll be looking at the change you're engaged in, and drawing it in detail so you can see it clearly. You'll be bringing into awareness what you'll be leaving behind as you leave your job (or your current approach to it), as you start doing new work in the world, work that comes from purpose. As you define and step into the work you're meant to do, whom are you becoming? What is taking shape within you? The more you can see, acknowledge, and experience the changes happening inside you, the more effective you will be.

You'll find that there's an old story you're moving out of, and a new story you're moving into. Your old story of who you are contained limitations that you're now moving beyond, and ways of thinking and being that no longer serve you. Your new story is the new paradigm you're moving into. Your new story is made up of new beliefs about what is possible, what you are capable of, and what you are willing to experience. It's important to mark the transition you're going through and experience it fully. This is how you create new brain pathways!

You Get to Lovingly Leave Your Baggage Behind

Before anyone goes through a big change or transition like the one you're going through, they have an Old Story. It's how they have seen themselves and the world, and the meaning they create out of it all. After their transition, when they reach the other side and make the changes that required them to transform personally, they have a New Story. It's their new way of looking at themselves and the world, and the new way they choose to interpret it.

The Old Story got them to where they were before the change. Where they were was exactly what the Old Story was capable of creating. Their New Story is what will carry them into the new way of being in the world, where their dream comes true. Only a New Story can create a new outcome like this.

Your old story includes all the things your saboteurs made up about you. It includes your assumptions about what wasn't possible for you or for the world. It includes all the heavy, saggy energy you felt every time you entertained new possibilities. It includes stories you made up about who you are and what kinds of things you can and cannot do. Your old story is an entire mental environment you created for yourself, using past experiences, traumas, internalized criticism or rejection, and all the meaning you made of it.

For example, I once had a client who was obviously incredibly creative – creativity ran through her bones – it wasn't as if it was just a hobby. She was a creative thinker and soul. And yet, this client had a story in her head that *I can't get inspired.* She told herself that she wasn't a person who could "envision." To her, it seemed true. She had all the evidence and past struggles to prove it. But it wasn't true that she couldn't envision. What was more likely true was that she'd been telling herself a story that she couldn't, so she stopped noticing that she did have the ability. Then she stopped trying.

I knew it because in so many areas of her life she *did* envision and she manifested like *crazy*! She was a powerful creator. She created all over the place! This story was attached to just one part of her identity, the one that had some wounded parts coloring her thinking. When I took her into dream mode for this part of her life, her vision came to the surface in about fifteen minutes.

We create stories to make sense of things, but so often we're wrong. If you hear yourself telling a story that begins with "I can't…" I urge you to catch yourself, take it back, and investigate. Remember, part three of this book is about choosing to act on your belief in possibility. Well, it goes both ways. When we choose to act on a belief in a story like this, we create the story in real life. We make it true. Don't make your false, negative stories about yourself true. Please don't spend your energy creating that. Make the story of your dream true. You'll be freer, happier, more empowered, and way more available and helpful to others in the end.

Change Really Does Happen and You're Generating It Right Now

Your New Story is the one you're building now. So far, it's filled with pictures, feelings, and sound bites of what you dream of. It has statements about your purpose that resonate viscerally with you. It has visions of the impact you want to make on others. It includes awareness of the impact you already make on others, without thinking, and your willingness to use this impact for good. Your new story includes your ability to create what you want from any circumstance, so that you're never stuck in victim mode, thinking that you have no control. You always have control, in that you can always make choices that affect how you experience what's happening and how you choose to move forward.

To create your New Story, all you have to do is take the vision you have, and always choose to move toward it. You simply accept the new ways of thinking that will get you there, and leave behind the ways that won't. For example, I used to have a story that because I was creative and sensitive, it was extra hard for me to find a line of work in which I would be valued. I'd heard so many times that artists can't make a living being artists. My dad told me on about ten different occasions the story of Michigan artist Charles Culver, who died because he couldn't make money. Now, that wasn't true. Charles Culver did die, but the rest of that story was something my dad made up on his own, based on his own stories of the way the world works. Because of these stories, which I internalized, I had major hang-ups about being able to make money – and have any value at all – as a creative person!

It was when I found coaching and my leadership training and community that I owned a new story. During those years, I uncovered layer upon layer of my value as a person, as well as value I was great at delivering, in both personal and work contexts. I owned it all. My story changed. Looking back afterword, I couldn't believe that I'd been blind to so much – all the talent, good, and wisdom inherent in my creativity and my sensitivity. It was always there, but the story in my head that I had about myself made it all invisible to me.

Trust that a new story is building for you. You may still think it's impossible to do the kind of work you want to do. It may still seem like a pipe dream to you. But the dream only seems unreal because you haven't lived it yet. If you choose to act on your belief in possibility, over and over, you will get there. And you'll realize that the feeling of impossibility was only one perspective. It wasn't real.

Keep acting on your belief and trust, in big and small ways. Do anything and everything you can to keep your flame lit, to keep yourself inspired, and to keep engaging your strengths and values.

What Will You Do with All Your New Skills?

You Have a Way to Stay Above the Fray

Now, you don't have to let stress or self-talk keep you from creating the work you want, and being who you want to be. You can identify when a saboteur has taken over and you're not at your best (and connect with your purpose to get grounded again). You know how to create what you want by dreaming first, rather than reacting mindlessly in stress. You know to revisit your purpose to gain strength and focus. You know to come back to heart-based emotions like appreciation and gratitude if you need to refresh your energy and feel expansive again.

You'll use these tools to move yourself from one place to another – from disempowered, bored, and unhappy to creative, focused, and fulfilled. You'll do this by finding meaningful work for yourself. But you can also do this daily, at your current job, to make it more fulfilling to you in the meantime.

You Can Create What You Really Want

When it comes to your future and the job you want, you don't have to limit yourself to what you think you can get. You can look well beyond your own status quo, and create what you *really* want instead. By doing this, you'll make your journey sustainable because it will be fueled by a truly compelling vision. You'll bring out the best in yourself, because that is what it will take to allow your vision come to life. The journey toward your goal will be every bit as satisfying as achieving the goal itself.

Because you've learned the importance of dreaming up what you want to happen, with just about anything you do, you'll find yourself more grounded. When you know where you're going, it's easier to make decisions.

You Can Enjoy Deep and Heart-Filled Motivation

Now that you are clear on your purpose and know to follow that seed of visceral clarity within you, you'll be able to maintain your motivation through the ups and downs of life. Purpose puts your two feet on the ground, and pulls you through mud and water when you need it to. Connecting to your purpose on a daily basis and knowing why you do what you do will allow you to then feel fulfilled by the process of getting there. This is true when it comes to you finding work you love, but it's also true when applied to your everyday to-do list. There is a reason for everything we do, even the stuff we resist or are bored by. When that reason is clear – when you understand the whole of what you are creating by completing that action – you will feel willing and open to it.

Your purpose is about who you are and what you care about most in the world, and it's also about something much bigger than you. Because of this, you can expect your purpose to take you places you didn't think you could go. It will grow you beyond what you think you're capable of, because it matters to you, if fulfills you, it makes you feel stronger, and because it will make you less attached to your ego.

You Can Surprise Yourself by Rising to Big Occasions

By using commitment as a tool to keep moving yourself forward, you'll grow to understand how resilient and agile you are. You'll watch yourself rise to the occasion, over and over, and this is how you will gain true confidence as a change-maker. You'll be aware that you don't know what challenges are ahead, but you'll also know that you have what you need to get through them. You can handle what comes your way.

In this way, you'll know exactly how to commit to possibility and you'll know what it's like to have conviction about a positive outcome. This will make you a better leader, because you'll embrace change more openly and readily. You'll know you are a change-maker.

You Can Revel in Your Inner Resources

By acknowledging your magic, and knowing that you have what you need right now to make a positive impact, you'll be able to relax into who you are and enjoy the resources already within you. From this place, you can receive appreciation and acknowledgment, you can begin to trust that part that carries the most light inside you. You'll be able to revel in the joy that brings, and feel the courage to be seen. You'll know that you don't need to strive to become someone you're not; you only need to settle more deeply into who you already are.

When you see and own your own magic, you'll see the magic in others. This will open your eyes to the good that surrounds you, so you can *receive* and *enjoy* it. This will in turn help you to sustain your energy, hope, and passion. Seeing the magic in others, you'll be able to keep your focus on what is good and workable. You'll be able to choose to bring out the best in others, and forgive their worst. You'll become a magnet for heart-based emotions, which will make those around you feel safe, welcomed, and engaged.

You'll not only keep your own focus on what is workable and possible, but you'll help everyone around you do the same. Collaboration will get easier, more playful, and more fulfilling.

You Can Always Keep Moving Toward Your Next Dream

By now, you understand that the tools that will help you find meaningful work aren't limited to applying for jobs. Knowing that action is a tool you can use to keep your engagement high, your commitment deepening, and your learning escalating, you'll have what you need to make sure the job you're applying for is the right one. You'll also ensure that when you get to that interview, you'll be showing up as the deeply committed and passionate self you really are.

Action is a creative process. You can always step into a perspective of play and experimentation to keep yourself moving forward. You are the creator of your life and your experiences. Things are never completely beyond your control. You always have choices. Actions is a way of creating what you choose, and choosing to create what you want.

You Can Use Challenges to Supercharge Your Growth

Alas, you're human. You'll have moments where you don't know how you'll get through the next challenge. You'll have slumps of doubt. You'll face situations where there is no right answer. You'll get your heart broken just because you care. All of these will be fuel for your growth. Because you know that any situation can be used for (and exists for the sake of) growing you into the person you want to be, you don't have to let those barriers stop you. In fact, you can use them to propel you.

You're a change-maker. You're not on this path because you want the easy road. You're on this path because you want to feel alive, and well used, and you want to make a difference in the world. Change-makers are leaders. They dig deep to rise to the occasion, and they know themselves well. Change-makers aren't afraid of being challenged. Change-makers will question themselves so they can become better at what they do. Change-makers choose to be conscious over being comfortable. Change-makers find comfort knowing they can create change.

Because you know you can use whatever barriers show up to help you create your vision, you won't be stopped. And in the process, you'll model strength of leadership to those around you.

You Are Becoming a Leader for Change

All of the skills you've learned in this chapter will take you from where you from where you are now – stuck, exhausted, and distracted – into clarity around your purpose and knowing how to create a life around it. You know that to create any change, you must:

- Believe it is possible,
- Believe you are capable, and
- Choose to act on those beliefs.

By incorporating each of the skills explored in these chapters, you'll be able to take responsibility for the changes you want by becoming the person who creates them. What I want you to know and remember, however, is that you can apply these steps to creating *any* change. You are becoming a change-maker, not just a job-finder. Practicing your ability to make change in your own life will give you the experience and conviction to lead change well beyond yourself.

What changes do you want to see in the world? I encourage you to dream big. Where do you see yourself making the biggest difference? What changes around you do you most want to make? Apply the three steps I listed above to these changes. Work with your belief that they are possible. Work with your belief in your own capacity to contribute to them. Then, choose to act on those beliefs.

You are a change-maker. We are all creating our world each day. You have the power to change it in positive ways, and if you found this book, you're being called to step forward. There's a reason for everything, and you are the reason I've written this book. On the other side is the world you dream of.

Acknowledgements

In 2015, I learned the true value of asking for help. Nothing scary that's worth doing has ever been done in a vacuum. I've come to understand that there are seen and unseen resources all around us, in every moment, for us to lean into. I've grown more and more comfortable leaning into them, and as a result, I've become more courageous and grounded in the midst of change, and vastly more fulfilled.

I'd like to first thank Angela Lauria, for creating the program in which I wrote this book. Angela, this has been the most useful (and brilliant) structure in which not only to become an author, but to step into a role of service with firmer conviction and a more committed heart. Thank you for all the professional and personal work you've done, to become the person who offered this program. Thank you, also, for knowing how to help me become the person who wrote this book.

More hearty thanks goes to Morgan James Publishing, for taking this book- and books like mine- and making them visible and available to the people who will most benefit from them by placing them in bookstores. I applaud your commitment to authors with hearts of service and am grateful for the opportunity to work with you. To the Morgan James Publishing team: Special thanks to David Hancock, CEO & Founder for believing in me and my message. To my Author Relations Manager, Aubrey Kosa, thanks for making the process seamless and easy. Many more thanks to everyone else, but especially Jim Howard, Bethany Marshall, and Nickcole Watkins.

Thank you to Maggie McReynolds, Grace Kerina and my line editors at the Author Incubator for their expertise, suggestions and corrections. When it came to finishing this project, you made everything easier.

I'd also like to thank my Tribe of Swallows. I'm lucky enough to enjoy the company of 20 or so close leadership comrades. We've grown together, gotten real together, and continue to support one another in our endeavors to create a positive impact in the world. In many ways, these people are my family. I thank you, Swallows, for being who you are, and for helping me see who I am. Special thanks to Nancy Yannett for your generous encouragement and insight, thank you Mary Barrett for your heart-based help processing big decisions, thank you Michael Wallace for always championing me and for contributing your poem to my book, thank you Stas Burdan for believing in me and my vision and for our Saturday get-togethers, thank you Tracey Abbott for your insights while developing my program. Thank you, *to all the Swallows,* for being in my world. I love you.

I want to take a moment to honor the Coaches Training Institute at which I trained to be a life coach and leader. CTI has changed countless lives, and empowered coaches across the world to help people change their lives, relationships, and organizations. My book is heavily influenced by my training, as well as my life experiences since that training began. I want to give a shout out to the magical coaches who have inspired me and made the greatest impact on me, including Gail Barrie, Pat House, and L.A. Reding. Your courage as coaches has become my gold standard, my model.

Thank you to my clients, for allowing me to share your stories in my book. I am the luckiest coach to have such pure-hearted, inspiring clients who want to blast through their self-perceived limits for the sake of themselves and others. I'm grateful to know you and watch you evolve.

Lastly, I'd like to thank my family. Special thanks go to Dad, for modeling such confidence in business, and for your interest and support. Thank you, Mom, for modeling for me – ever since I can remember – how to relax and just be with my creativity. And to Joe, Shu-Hui, Aimee, and Vernon, thanks for producing the cutest, most inspiring nieces an auntie could ever wish for.

About the Author

Julie is a Certified Professional Co-Active Coach and CTI-Trained Leader. She works with emotionally intelligent women who are compelled to create change in the world. Through her private coaching and programs, Julie helps clients free themselves from the frustration of a poor job-fit and uncover their true purpose, so they can do work that means something to them.

Client transformations have included:

- Leaving a paper-pushing role at work to start a law practice, co-found an NGO, and become an international leader in the activist community
- Going from stuck in a job with a limited future and a pattern of failed interviews, to landing their dream job
- Successfully moving from an administrative role to leading a change-initiative within the same company

Having spent decades searching for work that both fulfilled her and matched her potential, Julie encountered a life crisis which made her realize her calling. The journey she began as a result demystified what it takes for a sensitive empath to know her purpose, overcome confusion and doubt, and create the work she dreams of.

Julie believes that successfully creating change for ourselves is the first step to knowing how to also lead change in the world. Her mission is to awaken emotionally gifted, high-empathy women who long for more fulfillment and satisfaction at work to their change-making potential. A crisis of boredom and disillusionment is the perfect place to start that change.

An author, coach, leader, and artist, Julie lives in Boston, regularly walking the nearby woods with her goofball puppy.

website: julieboyercoaching.com

email: julie@julieboyercoaching.com

Thank You

Thank you for reading *Just Give Me Meaningful Work; Leave Your Exhausting Job and Start Making a Difference!*

I'd love to help you find work that means something to you, so you can enjoy life and feel great about what you do.

Looking for next steps? I've created a webinar for you to get you started on your journey. Email me at julie@julieboyercoaching.com with "Give Me Meaningful Work" in the subject line, and I'll send you the link!

Morgan James
Speakers Group

We connect Morgan James published authors with live and online events and audiences who will benefit from their expertise.

Morgan James makes all of our titles available
through the Library for All Charity Organization.

www.LibraryForAll.org

CPSIA information can be obtained
at www.ICGtesting.com
Printed in the USA
BVHW07s0852030718
520693BV00001B/4/P